# IT'S
# YOUR
# LIFE

# IT'S YOUR LIFE

---

*Your results ARE YOUR CHOICE*

---

## BY: NAVEED ASIF
## &
## SONIKA MADARASMI ASIF

Passion To Profit Publishing
Montreal, Quebec, Canada

**Library and Archives Canada Cataloguing in Publication**

Asif, Naveed, author
    It's your life: your results are your choice / by: Naveed Asif
& Sonika Madarasmi Asif.

Issued in print and electronic formats.
ISBN 978-0-9936843-4-0 (paperback).--ISBN 978-0-9936843-5-7 (pdf)

1. Self-realization. I. Madarasmi Asif, Sonika, author II. Title.

BF637.S4A75 2016                    158.1                    C2016-900001-X
                                                             C2016-900002-8

Passion To Profit Publishing
Montreal, Quebec, Canada
Cover Design by:
Gordan Blazevic (gordan.blazevic@gmail.com)

# Endorsements

"Emotionally charged and beautifully written! This book will appeal to anyone who has a desire to bring more depth and meaning to the results that they want to achieve."

**Danielle Joworski, Author of The ATHENA Prodigies: Empowering Women Empowering Girls**

It's Your Life is an extremely well designed, thought-provoking and brilliant book that I highly recommend. If there is something you want, and you have a burning desire, these authors will tell you precisely how to get there. Read, study and apply and watch amazing things happen in your world.

**Peggy McColl**
**New York Times Best-Selling Author"**

Naveed and Sonika have written truly beautiful piece of work. Once I started reading I couldn't put it down. They communicate so clearly and effectively the message that in order to change your results you must change your thinking. It is a must read for everyone who wants to make a major shift in their life. Within the pages are lessons and suggestions that help you understand and apply some very simple and practical steps. They have shared some of their own delightful stories of their own paths towards success which are truly inspiring. This book is a great read and full of wonderful information to help those who want to live a better life.

**Helen Rankin**
**Founder of Day Spa at Home**

It's YOUR life, and you should treat it like one! If you've ever wanted more from life than mediocrity, then this book is a must read! The way that Naveed & Sonika lay out their thoughts and ideas and then perfectly tie them in with real world (and relatable) stories from their lives is nothing less than brilliant. Don't wait any longer. Pick up your copy today!

**Jason Chechik**
**Small Business Marketing Expert,**
**International Best Selling Author**

# Dedication

This book is dedicated to our mentors Bob Proctor and Sandra Gallagher, as well as everyone else at the Proctor Gallagher Institute, who have shown us the way and given us the courage to break free and express our infinite potential.

# About The Authors

## NAVEED ASIF

Being born in Bangkok, Thailand, Naveed has inherited the culture of being compassionate towards people and helping them. During his days studying in university, he was asked by his father to join the family business part time, which gave him the fundamentals on how to operate a business. While working in his family business, he joined a networking marketing company in the Wellness industry. This decision changed his thinking forever because he got exposed to the concept of building freedom and earning passive income to have no financial concerns what so ever.

When Naveed began realizing his passion was to help others, he also realized he had to grow as a person in the process, in order to have massive breakthrough results. Therefore, he joined a self development course called The Landmark Forum. He then joined several seminars by T. Harv Eker – such as, Millionaire Mind Intensive, The Guerrilla Business Intensive, Train the Trainer, and Freedom Trader. These courses shifted his financial blueprint and he began a Forex trading business and started his own business along with several other online businesses.

However, his results were never consistent; this led him to The Secret, and eventually some more of Bob Proctor's videos and teachings. For the first time ever, Naveed understood that to change outside results, he needs to shift his inner world. Naveed made up his mind that no matter what it takes, he's going to work with Bob and teach people all around the world how to achieve phenomenal results. Today, Naveed is helping people locally and globally transform their lives like night and day.

## SONIKA MADARASMI ASIF

Born and raised in Bangkok, Thailand, Sonika was always known as one of the smartest kids in school. She had all the A+'s, teachers loved her, students copied her homework and everyone thought she would grow up to work in a top position at a large company. Sonika, however, never believed in conformity – she knew she would only do something if she set her heart on it. She broke her first barrier by attending Academy of Art University in San Francisco to complete her Bachelor of Fine Arts in Fashion. She then went on to work at many fashion jobs: fashion stylist, model booker, fashion magazine column writer, and production assistant; but she never experienced that intense feeling of inspiration.

Sonika quickly realized that the 9-5 lifestyle wasn't for her. She wanted freedom, and she wanted others to live the life of their dreams exactly the same way. After marrying her husband Naveed in 2014, Sonika began her journey in personal development. She attended the Landmark Forum, Landmark Advanced Course, as well as T.Harv Eker's online courses – but nothing clicked.

After watching The Secret, Sonika knew this information was exactly what she was missing, and she dove deeper into Bob Proctor's teachings. For the first time in her life, she felt a burning desire to do something bigger than she's ever done – and that something was to meet Bob Proctor, become a master at what he teaches and share this information with the world. Today, Sonika is living the life of her dreams by helping people all around the world break out of that 9-5 rut and finally enjoy this beautiful journey called life.

# Foreword

Like millions of people around the world, Naveed and Sonika Asif spent years trying to find and follow their passion, their path in life.

Naveed went from working in his family business, to network marketing, to developing a passion for helping others. Sonika attempted to work at many fashion jobs, but after a while she realized fashion wasn't really her passion. She wanted to help people achieve their goals.

Naveed and Sonika ended up taking self-development courses, and now they're both certified consultants helping their clients all around the world achieve their dreams and get the results they want.

Sonika and Naveed didn't achieve their dreams by happenstance. They did it by understanding and living in harmony with Universal Laws.

I've always loved the law. I knew from a very young age that I'd be a lawyer when I grew up and that's exactly what I did. And I enjoyed a very successful career as a banking attorney for an amazing 22 years.

Although I knew an awful lot about manmade laws back then, I didn't learn much about Universal Laws until I met Bob Proctor in 2006. Learning about these laws changed my way of thinking.

Now I study and live Universal Laws, such as the Law of Attraction and the Law of Success, every day. And even though things were pretty darn good when I was a lawyer, now I can honestly say that my life keeps getting better and better every day.

The same is true for Naveed and Sonika. Their lives are better now than ever before.

In It's Your Life, Naveed and Sonika not only share their stories, they share the ideas and principles that have gotten them where they are today. They also offer several exercises that helped them grow into their dreams.

Reading this book will be great for you to see practical examples of how you can apply the principles that Bob and I teach to your goals, your dreams, your life—just like Naveed and Sonika did.

If you have ever wondered if the principles you read about in personal development books and programs work for everyday people, you're going to love reading Naveed and Sonika's story. And if you're interested in making your life more than a formality, don't wait. Read this book.

**Sandy Gallagher**

# Table of Contents

# Introduction

"For most people, it's just a formality
when their hearts stop beating,
— because they never truly lived."
- Bob Proctor

The greatest minds in history have disagreed on virtually everything, but if there's one thing they all agreed on, it`s that we become what we think about.

It's Your Life is a product of endless conversations, brainstorm sessions and the passion to learn as much as possible from the world's greatest prosperity teacher: Bob Proctor. Our journey into the personal development industry began with a phone call that would forever change our lives. This book is a compilation of our life stories, everything we have learned and more, all aimed at enhancing the reader's awareness and aiding his/her creation of a beautiful and prosperous life.

The book is filled with exercises for the reader to engage in directly, as well as entertaining and emotional moments from our own lives which we hope will impart true knowledge to the reader. We encourage the reader to allow their imagination to flow as they progress through this book, and follow/complete all the available suggestions and exercises.

We have used every single tool shared in this book in our own lives, and our aim is to share this information with millions of people all around the world who are looking for a chance to improve their lives.

# PART I:

# The Grey Area

CHAPTER 1

# A Good Compass

**S** onika: *Back when I was 8 years old, I had a pretty traumatic experience (well it was probably traumatic because I was only 8 years old). I was in a shopping mall with my parents and we were on the escalator, and as we approached the bottom, I saw a fish tank on my right. I was immediately drawn to its colorful presence, and stopped to take a look. Wide-eyed, I cupped my hands around my face and peered into the fish tank. I saw blue stripes, red scales and yellow fins. It felt like only 5 minutes had gone by, but when I turned around my parents had disappeared. 'They couldn't have gone very far,' I thought to myself, but every passing second felt like an eternity. I started to panic and ran towards the middle of the aisle and stood there, frantically searching through the crowd. Images flashed in my mind of everything I had learned from school about what to do when you get lost. And suddenly, I knew exactly what to do. I trusted those images in my mind and I stood there, calming myself down. Rule #1: Stay where you are so they know where to find you. Rule #2: Figure out where you are so you know what to do in order to get where you want to go. I stood there, and turned in all directions: North, South, East and West. I realized I was in the perfume and makeup area of the mall. I was just starting to look for someone who could help, when a lady walked up to me and asked me what my name was and why I was alone. I told her I couldn't find my parents, and she told me she would help me and took my hand. At that very moment, I heard my mom call my name from behind. I turned around and there she was. I realized in that moment, that if I hadn't figured out where I was, I wouldn't have known what to do, and we all would have probably run around frantically for the next hour trying to find each other."*

5

Just like that 8-year-old in the story, we first need to know *where* we are and *who* we are in order to figure out where we want to go. This is probably the hardest question to answer: **Who Am I?** This is the greatest challenge most people face, because they don't know who they are, and they aren't even aware that they don't know.

Our mentor, Bob Proctor, has been reading *Think and Grow Rich* by Napoleon Hill for over 50 years. The man who gave Bob this book was Raymond Douglas Stanford. Raymond asked Bob 'Who are you?' and with confidence Bob replied, 'Well, I'm Bob.' When Raymond replied, 'That's not you, that's just your name,' Bob wasn't sure what he meant. So he pointed to himself and said, 'Well this is me.' Once again, Raymond disagreed and said 'that's just your body.' In that moment, Bob realized that Raymond was trying to get him to understand who he was; because that was the only way he would be able to change the results he was getting in life. **If you want to change your results, you better know who you are.**

We go through almost 20 years of education, yet we never graduate knowing who we really are. If there's one thing we know, based on numerous years of research, it's this: *We are spiritual beings, we live in a physical body, and we have an intellect.* If you look at yourself under a microscope, you will realize that you are a molecular structure in a very high frequency of vibration. You are simply energy in constant and rapid motion. Give this a shot: close your eyes and visualize the inside of your skull. Now slowly move downward towards your neck, keep going until you reach your stomach. Visualize the inside of your legs and your feet. Now bring yourself all the way back up to the inside of your skull. The reason you can visualize and travel through and around your body is simply because *you* are not your body; you're just locked in one.

Ralph Waldo Emmerson once said, 'A man becomes what he thinks about all day long.' You are who you are because of your thoughts. You are at a certain frequency of vibration because of your thoughts. If we want to get better results, we need to be in a frequency of vibration that is positive, one that is in the same frequency as the results we want to achieve - one that we *love*.

## Your Burning Desire

What puts you in a positive vibration? What are some things that you really want to achieve in life? Now you may *think* that you really want something, but there's a reason that result is not manifesting in your life. There is a difference between a simple wish, and a burning desire.

Napoleon Hill, author of *Think and Grow Rich*, perfectly described how desire is the first step required for making your dreams come true. He said, 'The starting point for all achievement is desire. Keep this constantly in mind. Weak desires bring weak results; just as a small fire makes a small amount of heat.' Strong desires are the only ones that manifest into the results that we're truly passionate about.

**Naveed:** *"When I was in 5<sup>th</sup> Grade, I was told that I could select any extra class of my choice. I decided to take a class on acoustic guitar. At this point I had no idea how to play a single note, let alone formulate a simple melody like 'Mary Had a Little Lamb'. But I wasn't afraid; in fact, I was excited. There was something seeking expression from within, I felt illuminated at the thought of one day playing notes like Jimmy Hendrix. I didn't care how difficult it was going to be, or how long it would take, I just knew I would one day play like him. There I was on my first day, holding a guitar for the first time. When my instructor taught me the formation and my fingers pressed firmly onto the metal strings, it felt as though they were piercing through my skin. It was one of the most painful experiences I had ever had, and it didn't get any easier. I had calluses and cuts all over my fingers. That desire to learn, however, never stopped. I kept at it until I could finally hold the chord successfully. Then I took it to the next level by buying an electric guitar. After 6 years of trials and errors, practicing 28 hours a week, I was finally able to play some of Hendrix's best pieces.*

We live our life on a day-to-day basis, wishing for a different outcome. We dream about turning our hobbies into our careers, we sit and think about the person we want to spend the rest of our life with. We know *what* we desire, but how do we achieve it? This is where we can differentiate between that fire - that burning desire - from simple wishes. **The way to know that you have a burning desire is simply to look at the way you are pursuing it.** If you are being cautious, and attempting to make it safely to your destination, your desire is nothing more than a whisper of hope.

## Desire is Nothing More Than an Accurate Picture

Desire causes frustration for a lot of people, due to ignorance and lack of knowledge about why and how it relates to human nature. According to Earl Nightingale, **desire is nothing more than an accurate picture of what you will one day become.** If we truly study what we feel when we visualize a desire, we will come to understand that we would not be longing for certain things if we weren't able to achieve them. Claude Adrien Helvetius (1715-1771), was a French philosopher during the Age of Enlightenment; an era filled with cultural and intellectual forces which emphasized reason, analysis and individualism. Helvetius understood the mechanisms of the human mind, and he came to realize that 'by annihilating the desires, you annihilate the mind [itself].' The mind cannot live without desire, as it's a part of the natural laws of the universe. Desire is energy, and the mind is simply transforming this energy into a form that we can understand.

Everything in nature is perfectly timed, perfectly accurate, and our desires are no exception. Ralph Waldo Emerson thoroughly understood the *purpose* of desire. He said that 'There's nothing capricious in nature, and the implanting of a desire indicates that its gratification is in the constitution of the creature that feels it.' In other words, nature doesn't have mood swings or operate randomly: flowers don't coincidentally bloom every spring; animals don't randomly hibernate during winter. There is always a reason for existence and our desires exist simply because we are able to achieve them in physical reality.

## Desire Can Outwit Mother Nature

We've heard many stories about miraculous situations like when a mute child begins to talk, or when people who are clinically dead come back to life, and those who seem to have hit rock bottom rise to become one of the greatest legends in history.

These stories shock us; we're completely taken aback by them and we applaud these men and women for their accomplishments. But, 10 minutes later we go back to doing exactly what we were doing. The next day, it's even worse. We don't even remember the names of those people or what they did.

You can inspire your friends a million times with Donald Trump's accomplishments; you can tell your son over and over again about how his cousin is now so successfully and energetically studying to become a doctor. They will definitely be inspired, but only for those few moments when they're listening to you. Here's the reason: they're not interested.

Have you noticed that when we really like what we're doing, we're that much better at it? A child can be a master at video games, but fail in science class. Why does this happen? He's provided with all the necessary information in school. Why is he failing? He didn't know how to play the video game when he first bought it; he had to *learn* how to do that. Yet - unlike science - he started to excel.

The answer is that he became a master at playing video games because he had the DESIRE to do so. You may say, 'well video games are fun, it's not surprising that he put all that energy into learning how to play them.' You're absolutely right. He was having FUN. He had the DESIRE to play and the PASSION to improve. That's why it became so easy. Find something you have a passion for, and watch how quickly you achieve your goals!

Napoleon Hill, in *Think and Grow Rich*, stated that 'Desire backed by faith knows no words such as impossible.' When you have a burning desire to do something, you don't know what Plan B is. You don't understand the word 'Failure'. All you have is your vision, your intentions and the fact that you believe - beyond a shadow of a doubt - that you are going to reach your goal. So many human beings suppress their burning desires and let their rational minds take over, thinking; 'I don't have time', 'It's too risky', 'I don't have the money to do something like that.' Then these very people wonder why they aren't getting the results they want.

These beliefs become so engrained in their minds that they begin to believe that money is hard to earn and that some people are just destined to be poor. They fall into a rut, with no hope of ever finding their way out.

There's no reason to wait for your dreams to come true. Waiting for money to start a business, or waiting for that perfect moment to begin a new health routine, is like waiting for your muscles to grow before you decide to pick up a dumbbell - it's never going to happen. James Allen said 'If your real desire is to be good, then there is no need to wait for the money before you do it. You can do it now, this very moment, just where you are.' Take action NOW.

Great men didn't become great by listening to naysayers and doubters. Rich men didn't become rich by staying at a job they hated. They became who they are because they had an idea - an idea that created a burning DESIRE in their minds, their hearts and their souls. This desire is what drove them to begin their journey to abundance.

The universe has everything you need to succeed. According to Bob

Proctor, a legend in the personal growth industry and author of *You Were Born Rich*, the resources you need to make your dream come true are already available to you. The resources needed to create the Internet were always available, we just needed to *know how* to use them to create it, and now we have. But it started with an idea, which translated into a DESIRE to turn the internet into a physical reality. Once that step was achieved, even Mother Nature couldn't stop it from manifesting.

Doctors have told so many people they will never walk again, but this is just an opinion! Neither doctors nor anyone else truly know what you're capable of. If you can allow yourself to let go of all your doubts, and embrace your desire of walking on two feet once again, the universe will come to your aid and give you everything you need.

Don't let anyone tell you that you can't do something. Only listen to your desires and follow in the footsteps of those who have achieved such great goals. They had an idea and they acted on it. Pick up those dreams and feel that burning desire in you to do what you REALLY WANT TO DO. Because those desires are the key to helping you achieve the results you truly want.

## How to Turn Up The Heat On Your Burning Desire

Before turning up the heat, you first need to know what your desires are. The first step is to recognize that you have them. It may be that you've been shoving it into the back of your mind for years. Desires are created by exercising our imagination, but we'll get into this higher faculty later on in the book. For now, we'd just like you to think back to your childhood. What toys and games did you play with, what books did you read? Did something resonate with you that ignited your imagination? Did you ever pretend that you were a different person? Maybe you wanted to be a chef cooking with your toy stove, or a super hero dressed up in a Superman costume. Really allow yourself to enjoy this nostalgic journey, because this is your chance to let reality go and really start using the creative part of your mind. Thomas Edison, the inventor of incandescent light, allowed his burning desires to take over through this exact exercise. He dove deep into the reservoirs of his deepest passions and pulled out an idea that he really wanted to make real. He stuck with it, through and through, and even though he failed over ten thousand times he never gave up. That is the difference between a burning desire and wishful thinking. The way you pursue a desire is vastly different from the way you pursue a job. A job can be something that helps you scrape by, or one that you think you love simply because you're told by other people that you're lucky to have it. Take a few minutes to really consider what you typically think about during the day? What do you think about when you wake up or when you go to bed? What do you do in your free time that you really enjoy and which - as a result - you're really good at? This is where your passion lies, and this is the key to your success. Keep building images of your dreams, as it is through this process that those dreams will turn into desires. As you keep reading, you will learn how to turn desire into your driving force in order to help you seamlessly achieve your goals.

# CHAPTER 2

# Naptime is Boring!

**S**onika: *Nap time; the good old days. It was the one thing I didn't look forward to in kindergarten, but took great advantage of in high school and college. I remember back in kindergarten, there was a bulletin board that had names of all the kids in the class, along with a blank strip of paper below each name. If we scored the highest on any assignment or helped one of our peers (basically if we did anything right), we were awarded a gold star. At the end of the semester, the person with the highest number of stars would get rewarded. Of course, I won it for the entire year. I wouldn't allow it to be any other way. But if there was one thing that I didn't want a gold star for, it was naptime. Oh, how I hated it! An hour before the school day was over, all the lights were turned off and we were forced into our Minnie Mouse blankets. I remember the uneasy adrenaline rush that flowed through my body every time I was forced to go to sleep at 1 P.M. I would toss and turn, fake sleep, or kick my blanket off altogether. As you may have guessed, I never got a gold star for naptime. But if there was one thing that made these moments easier, it was my ability to daydream. I pictured leaving school and going home to my pet dog, Simba, or running around in my neighborhood with my friends. I would build beautiful shapes, colors and images in my mind, waiting impatiently for the moment that I would be allowed to get up and splash them all onto a piece of paper. As I grew up, naptime became less frequent; but I began to crave it more. With the stress of homework, sports, graduation and exams, I longed for the days I could get rewarded for closing my eyes and sleeping for an extra hour every day. Today, coaching others through my Thinking Into Results program, I'm using my imagination the same way I used it when I was 6 years old. Doing what I love and living my dream, I definitely don't need naptime anymore!*

When we were little kids, we used our imaginations. We'd watch cartoons; we used to create sand castles and buildings using sand and cardboard. We used to create forts using pillows, and we didn't care that we were coloring outside the lines. We were free because we didn't know how to be any other way.

A few years later, everything changed. Those lines in our coloring books became a requirement, sand and cardboard were replaced with pens and rulers, and every time we let our minds wander, we were told to 'stop daydreaming and pay attention.' Pretty soon we were so focused on following directions, getting through school and conforming to our culture and society that we forgot about this amazing higher faculty.

You see, daydreaming is our way of exercising our imagination. Napoleon Hill, in his book 'Think and Grow Rich', stated that the 'imagination is the most marvelous, miraculous, inconceivably powerful force that the world has ever known.' Our imagination helps us build beautiful images in our mind, which we can then turn into a physical reality. Everything in our world today is the product of someone's imagination. This very book was a product of our imagination which we turned into a physical reality by following the very steps we are sharing with you.

As we grew up, we decided that imagination has no place in this realistic and logical world. We began to believe that using our imagination only made sense at times when we were having fun, or if our job required it. Think of multinational corporations today. They've got huge companies, but very tiny creative departments. People don't believe they are creative, which is far from the truth - it all depends on how much you've developed your creative abilities. We've all got it, and it's just a question of how much we're going to develop it. Pablo Picasso, a famous modern artist in the 20th century, said, 'Every child is an artist. The problem is how to remain an artist once he grows up.'

**Naveed:** *Back in middle school, we used to have a pep rally every year, an event where kids got together to play games and compete against each other. The theme this year was to dress up as our favorite character from pop culture (movies, TV, comics, etc...). I had less than 48 hours to decide which character I wanted to dress up as. So I went home and put myself into a completely relaxed state of mind, thinking of all the characters I really enjoyed watching on TV, and one that I would enjoy turning into for a whole day. Almost immediately an image of Wolverine, a character from the X-men movie, flashed in my mind. This character is a mutant, who has 3 metal* *claws that slide right out of his fist when he's ready to attack. It may sound silly, but when you're a kid you don't really care what people think, you just love the idea of becoming your favorite character. I had no idea how I would find a way to make it as realistic as possible in comparison to the actual movie, but I just knew one thing; that I wanted it, and I wanted it to be an exact replica. As I was brainstorming with my pencil and paper, I realized there was a magazine ad lying in the corner of my room, one that had a clear image of the metal claws in full detail. I grabbed the ad and took it to a carpenter who was working on our house at the time. I told him I wanted him to cut pieces of wood in the exact shape and length as was shown on that piece of paper. After giving him the exact measurements of my fingers (I needed them to rest nicely in between each finger), he went home and worked on it for me. The next day he showed me the exact copy of what was shown in the magazine. Now how could I give this a metallic look? I asked members of my family for advice. My dad likes to fix and revamp things in the house from time to time, so he had a collection of a lot of different materials, and he just happened to have exactly what I needed: Foil tape. I wrapped the foil tape around the wooden claws, and few minutes later, I had fake metal claws that looked identical to Wolverine's. The character also has side burns, which I obviously didn't as a 13-year-old boy. Fortunately, I found black sheep wool for that purpose. When the day of the pep rally arrived, I became the character I had always wanted to be and all my friends became obsessed with my claws. If I was older, I probably would've never thought I could create anything close to this exact of a replica of my favorite character, simply because I would've cared too much about what others thought to get anything done.*

The sole reason why things get done more easily when we're kids is because kids do not have the ability to say 'I can't', so they are able to figure things out. Their minds are still fresh and full of possibilities and imagination. However, the line between 'I can' and 'I can't' grows stronger as we grow older; because we have been told countless times that the word 'impossible' exists. Our imaginative faculty gets weaker each day the more we're told to 'stop dreaming and pay attention.'

If there's one thing all successful people know, it's that imagination is absolutely imperative. Your imagination is showing you where you want to go; it's showing you a picture, a preview of your desires! Albert Einstein, a famous theoretical physicist and Nobel Prize winner, was one of the world's most knowledgeable men when it came to the idea of imagination. Describing it perfectly, he stated that 'your imagination is your preview of life's coming attractions.' Einstein knew that painting a picture in your mind was required in order to prepare the action steps needed to proceed towards that dream. He understood that knowledge is about knowing what there is to know today, while our imagination is showing us all we ever will be able to know and understand. In other words, we stop becoming confined to our own rules and regulations when we begin to exercise our imagination.

## How to Develop Your Imagination

We've got energy that is flowing to and through us on a constant basis. In the 1930's a Russian photographer by the name of Semyon Kirlian perfected a form of photography that captured this beautiful energy leaving our body; today this form of photography is known as Kirlian photography. The more relaxed we allow ourselves to be, the more we attract this beautiful energy. This is where imagination truly begins.

'Visioneering' is simply another word for visualizing, but with a deeper meaning. It's an act of creating an image in your mind, one that truly matters to you, and getting emotionally involved with it. Our imagination is the faculty out of which visions arise. To truly experience this ability at its fullest, you have got to shut down your sensory factors and kick your imagination into high gear.

Begin by moving into a space where you feel 100% free and relaxed. Allow yourself to be away from everyone and everything; you might go sit under a tree somewhere, or on your terrace overlooking the city. Close your eyes and take a few deep breaths. Allow your body to totally relax and let go of any stressful thoughts. At this point, you are allowing energy to flow to and through every cell in your body.

Now let your mind wander; allow it to travel through space and time. Allow yourself to fully enjoy this exercise, as it isn't something we permit ourselves to do very often. Now that your imagination is in full swing, start imagining the life you truly desire. What kind of house do you want? What kind of person do you want to be? What is your dream job? Who is the person you want to spend your life with?

At this point, you will begin to attract the thoughts you need to make your life more enjoyable. Start to really see the life you want in its full detail and hold that image in your mind. You are starting to bring order to your desires and the life you want; you are now seeing it manifest in your very mind.

Where there is order, there is no hurry. Your mind and energy are now calm and relaxed. When we feel the need to hurry we are experiencing nervousness, which is a destructive emotion. It stems from worry and fear, and will only lead us to results that are negative.

All of us visualize, whether we know it or not - the problem is that most of us visualize and imagine what we don't want, and we end up living like that very image we hold in our minds. Vincent Van Gough, a famous artist during the Post-Impression period, said that 'I dream my painting and then I paint my dream.' Develop this amazing part of your intellect, paint beautiful pictures in your mind and live that way. As you get better at developing this imaginative ability, you will begin to attract the thoughts you need to move further into this process of manifestation.

CHAPTER 3

# A Progressive Realization

**Sonika:** *Sometimes I forget how many trials and errors I went through before I got to this point in my life; maybe because I barely lasted through any of my trials. I realized a few years ago, that if I wasn't in love with what I was doing, I wouldn't be good at it. A few years ago, I graduated with a degree in Fashion Merchandising. Choosing this major was a last minute decision that I made right before I graduated from high school. For 12 out of those 13 years of education, my heart was set on becoming a veterinarian, but as I explored the world of fashion toward the end of my education, I decided that was more of a passion for me. So I went off to college to pursue my BFA Fashion Merchandising degree. Now I had been brought up to believe that I needed to pursue a job in an industry related to my degree - just like a lot of other people. This belief was so strong that I didn't even consider looking for jobs in other industries. After graduation, I returned home and began a full-blown job search. I got a lot of job offers, and I selected one that I felt would give me a lot of experience. Here's what bothered me: after 4 years of hard work, projects, and portfolio building, I didn't utilize a single thing I had learned from my college education. Nothing! After 8 months, I decided to look for another job that would allow me to use more of the knowledge I had about the industry. So I went ahead and became a stylist for an online fashion company. When we hear the term stylist we think 'glamour', 'imagination' and 'creativity'. Now this may hold true if you're a celebrity stylist, or a stylist for a magazine, but for an online fashion company? Not a chance. I wasn't allowed to use my creativity to style any products, and I couldn't play with the background colors as they all needed to be plain white to display nicely on the website. So, as you can guess, I gave that job up as well. At this point I was truly searching for something that would allow me to express my passion* *and creativity, and I was willing to go out of my comfort zone and look for something in another industry. After a few more years of trial and error, I found my heart and soul as a Proctor Gallagher Institute Consultant. By coaching others through the Thinking Into Results program and building up my own knowledge about personal development, I realized that success is about the journey, not the destination. Even if I don't fully achieve my life goals, I know I'll have a happier and more prosperous journey than a lot of people who feel they have to stick with something they hate just to make ends meet.*

Earl Nightingale put it very well when he said that 'Success is the progressive realization of a worthy ideal.' They key word here is *progressive*. When we're pursuing a goal, a lot of us fail to be consistent. One day we're doing really well, and the next day we're making up excuses as to why we can't keep going. If you've got a goal that you're aiming for, and you're getting better every day (it doesn't matter if you're just growing your knowledge or taking action), you can go ahead and tell everyone around you that you're successful. That's it. That's all success is. So why is it that 1% of the population are earning 96% of all the money? With success being such a simple concept, why are so many people struggling to get by?

The reason is that **96% of the world's population are not pursuing their worthy ideal.** A worthy ideal is an idea that you have fallen absolutely in love with. If you've got someone in your life that you're in love with, think about what you would do for that person. You would break your bank account for them, you would fly across the world just to see them for a few hours, and no matter what the circumstance, you would find a way to get in touch with them. That's how you've got to be with your goal! That's your worthy ideal! You've got to be willing to do absolutely anything if it means you can achieve your goal. If you are not pursuing your worthy ideal, your journey towards success will never be progressive. That is a guarantee.

## The Worthy Ideal

Take a moment to think about your goals. How many goals do you have? What are they? Do your goals make you excited or afraid? Or do you seem to fall off track and get bored after a while? Keep these questions in mind as we progress through this chapter.

We've been setting goals our whole lives. It began when we wanted to learn how to walk, and when we wanted to get on a bike. As we grew older, our goal was to get behind the wheel of a car. Goals are like that. As we change and grow, our goals follow suit. Think back to when you were in school or college, and your biggest goal for the week was to finish your essay or project on time. You set deadlines each day, sometimes you were on time, and other times you fell off track.

After going through almost 20 years of school and education, we've all gotten into the habit of looking at goals as deadlines, and we usually set them based on the capacity we believe we can handle. This exact goal-setting process is applied to our careers, and by extension, our entire lives.

If you stop someone on the street and ask them what their goals are, chances are they won't know what you're talking about. Some might respond with a goal they want to achieve 3 days from now, while others will be completely dumbfounded. If they do have a goal, ask them if they've got it in writing, and again, chances are they won't.

Let's talk about the easiest type of goal we all set: A New Year's Resolution. We used to love setting New Year's Resolutions. We would both set fitness goals for the year, and we used to get so excited about it. But as February came along, we had forgotten all about it. This is a very common pattern for those who are not aware of an effective goal-setting process. Setting the right type of goal is the key to achieving your greatest desires. American author and motivational speaker Zig Ziglar once said, 'A goal properly set is halfway reached.' This simply means that if you've set the right goal, it's a guarantee that you're going to end up in the right place - that's half the battle.

Most people unfortunately don't understand the real purpose of having a goal. A majority of us think that the true purpose of a goal is to buy a new car, or get a new house. But these are just benefits, a result of setting your goals. **The true purpose of a goal is to grow.** We understand that there are 3 types of goals. The first one (let's call this Type-A Goals) is a goal that you know how to reach. This is usually a goal you've already achieved in the past, and can duplicate over and over again as needed. Our mentor, Bob Proctor, once told us a story about a student of his. He asked his student what his goal was, to which the student replied, 'I want to get a new Pontiac.' Bob asked him what he was currently driving, and his student replied that he was currently driving a Pontiac. Slightly confused, Bob went on to ask him how long he's had his car. The student said he's had it for 4 years, and he bought

NAVEED ASIF & SONIKA MADARASMI ASIF

it brand new 4 years ago. Now this student knew for 4 years how to get a new Pontiac, since he had already done so once in the past. This didn't constitute a goal, because a goal is something that you're going to go after that you've never achieved before.

The second type of goal (a Type-B Goal) is the one that the majority of us set on a daily basis, and that's a goal that you think you can reach. We've never done it before, but we've planned out exactly how we're going to achieve it. We had a client once, who told us that her goal was to find the money to pay for our Thinking Into Results program. 'If I do this, and then this happens, then I'll be able to join the program.' That's usually how the conversation goes. A person with this type of goal always has a solid plan on how they're going to achieve it.

Now the last type of goal is a fantasy, or a Type-C goal. It's a goal that you've dreamed about for years, and you can never sit down and figure out exactly how to achieve it, because it's so big and seems so far away. It's usually a goal that receives a lot of criticism from people around you, simply because there's no clear plan to back it up. It's a goal that excites and scares you at the same time. Bob Proctor once said that you need to 'set a goal to achieve something so big, so exhilarating that it excites you and scares you at the same time.' If you're going after your fantasy, you're going to have to stretch - you've got to break free of your comfort zone. You're going try to come up with a plan and attempt to find the necessary resources, and you're not going to be able to. You're not going to know the *How*. The fun is in figuring out the *How!* Mahatma Gandhi said, 'Glory lies in the attempt to reach one's goal and not in reaching it.' Your only choice is to look within and pull on something inside of you. Here lies the true purpose of a goal.

## How to Set Worthy Goals

Your first step is to understand that your goal has got to be a fantasy. It's what you've always wanted to do, but never found the courage to try and achieve. Allow your deepest desires to help you realize what you want, and then turn that desire into your goal. Now that you've got a list of the things you're really passionate about, choose one that you're most excited about. This is your burning desire.

Now when you have a fantasy in the back of your mind, it doesn't affect how you operate on a daily basis simply because you haven't played around with the idea. Well that's what we're going to do now.

20

Play around and think about how you would approach this goal; at this very moment your fantasy is turning into a theory. Your level of excitement and fear is going to kick into high gear at this point, but stay with it. The reason why you're excited is because on a conscious level this is what you want, but on a subconscious level, you're moving into a new area. We'll get into the subconscious mind and how it affects every moment of your life later on.

After discarding ideas about how you would approach this theory, you're going to ask yourself two questions. First, ask yourself 'Am I able to do this?' Before you answer, think about this: science and theology have taught us that nothing is ever created or destroyed, and that we're made up of a mass of molecules moving at a very high speed of vibration. We're big masses of energy, everything around us is energy. So if nothing is ever created or destroyed, all that we need is already available to us in one form or another. We've got enough energy locked up inside of us to light up an entire city for a week. That energy within us represents the amount of potential that we possess. You've got deep reservoirs of talent within you; in other words, you are very much ABLE to achieve your fantasy.

The second question you need to ask yourself is 'Am I willing?' Are you willing to do what it takes? Are you willing to pay the price? People often confuse ability with willingness. They tell themselves they aren't able to do something, but the truth is they simply aren't *willing* to take the necessary steps. We make excuses and say that our circumstances are the reason we can't do something. It's like Albert Einstein once said, 'If you want to live a happy life, tie it to a goal, not to people or things.' The only person who is going to break you out of your old cycle is you. Big risks and big goals come with a big price. The price to pay in most cases is money, opposition and time. Thomas Edison's biggest dream and desire was to create incandescent light. He was ridiculed by everyone he knew, because it was such an illogical idea at the time. Look around your home or your office right now. Today, it would be illogical to *not* have light bulbs in your ceiling. In the process of manifesting his dream, Edison failed over ten thousand times. He was willing to do that, if it meant he could fulfill his dream. If you're willing to do what it takes, you've got to give it your all.

Now there's a basic law of the universe that says 'create or disintegrate.' If you're not moving forward, you're going backwards. There's a reason why people who go after Type-A or Type-B goals end up quitting sooner rather than later. Here's the reason: **there's absolutely no inspiration in going after the first two types of goals,** absolutely none. We've discovered that people aren't as afraid of change, as they are of *being changed.* When you begin to transition up the ladder, from Type-A to Type-B goals, you're going to face some serious opposition. People around you aren't going to believe that you can achieve something way outside of their own conceptions, but when you have a Type-B goal, you can still assure them with your solid plans and step-by-step process. Now when moving from a Type-B goal to your Type-C goal, this opposing force from your environment and the people around you is going to get even stronger. You've overcome looking for the *How* at this point, and this makes no sense to anybody else. Your thinking and mindset have begun to shift, and your family and friends may not understand because they don't want you to change. If you drastically shift your old way of thinking away from theirs, they will then have to change and adapt to the new you; rest assured, people don't like being changed.

When you go after what you want, you're going to have no choice but to grow in order to reach a point you've never been able to in the past. Don't mess around with little goals. Now this doesn't mean you can't have small goals, as long as they're leading you up to your big one. Charles C. Noble, who was awarded the Army Distinguished Service medal for his actions during the Vietnam War, and possibly the best engineer of his time, once said, 'You must have long term goals to keep from being frustrated about short term failures.' Your big goal is going to keep you going; it will keep you motivated and bring true purpose to your life. Make sure what you're creating is big and beautiful, and then decide - right now - that this is what you want, and that nothing is going to hold you back.

CHAPTER 4

# Are You Willing & Able?

H enry Ford once said, 'Whether you think you can or can't, either way you are right.' It is inevitable that after selecting a fantasy goal, we are going to wonder whether we can really achieve that which we desire. Type-C goals exist in in the realm of multiple possibilities, most of which we are unaware of at this time. **A decision is a commitment that you make with yourself, your spirit and the universe that you are *willing* and *able* to do whatever it takes.**

We make decisions every day, but the majority of them don't have any significant impact on our results because our decisions are usually made within our comfort zone and the conditioning that we received from our parents and our environment. We want to tell you a little story about how we made the biggest decision of our lives, one that has brought us to a point that we will never turn back from.

A few months ago, we were scrambling between three different businesses: An e-commerce business, a Forex trading business, and an affiliate-based business. We were earning some money, but barely enough to get by. We had heard from various sources that it was a good idea to build multiple sources of income and that having Multiple Sources of Income (MSIs) is the difference between being rich and being wealthy. Therefore, we didn't truly understand why we weren't getting the results we wanted. We happened to join a live call by T. Harv Eker, a multi-millionaire business owner and #1 New York Time's bestselling author. During this call, Harv Eker said something that completely changed the course of our business. He told us a story about how he attempted to take on too many things at once and expand his income too quickly. As a result, he kept going broke, over and over again. He said he realized that 'what you focus on expands.' In other words, what you don't focus on is going to fall away, and if you do too many things at once, you will not provide the necessary focus to build one solid source of income. This segment of the call opened our eyes to all the reasons why weren't getting the results we wanted.

At this point, we were about to make two decisions. We were aware of the first decision, but still unaware of the second one at this point. Our first and most important decision was to cut out the businesses that we were not passionate about and the ones that were not providing us with a significant source of income. This decision was hard to make, not only because we were decreasing our income, but also because we had taken on the role of a mentor for a group of people in the trading industry. We sat back and realized we weren't giving them the value they deserved because this industry wasn't really our passion; therefore, we weren't studying and learning enough about it for it to benefit the members of our group. So we decided to finally give them the value they deserved by introducing them to a mentor who was more passionate and experienced. We did not make an affiliate commission on these referrals, but we did fulfill our responsibility by helping them reach their trading goals.

Our second decision did not come to us until a few weeks later. One day, in our spare time, we turned on a movie called *The Secret*. This was probably our tenth time watching this film, but for the first time the results of watching this film would be more profound than anything we could've imagined. Our mentor, Bob Proctor, is the first man that comes on screen in this movie. We were curious to learn what else he knew about acquiring and attracting your dreams. So we went on YouTube and watched several videos of his seminars, through which we got the inspired idea to visit his website and check out his other programs. Our eyes immediately went to his consultant certification program because it gave us a chance to go out there and share this knowledge with people all around the world.

What happened in that moment was extraordinary; we felt a rush of positive energy, and we knew we had found something that we wanted to do for the rest of our lives. We realized in that moment that throughout our careers, we enjoyed helping people succeed more than doing our actual jobs. This was a chance to help people for a living. We immediately signed up and as there was no price on the website, nothing stopped us from taking the step to talk to someone at the Proctor Gallagher Institute. Two weeks later, we got a call from one of the PGI representatives asking if we wanted to learn more about the program. After discussing our goals and dreams, we were smacked with a price that we couldn't afford - or so we thought. We hung up the phone and looked at each other; we knew we both wanted it, we could feel each other's energy. We did not talk to each other, we did not discuss it with anyone else, and we just took a leap of faith and made a decision. We picked up the phone and called PGI - two minutes later we gave them our credit card information.

At this point, we didn't realize that we were acting in the exact same way as successful people. According to Napoleon Hill, 'Successful people make decisions fairly quickly (as soon as the facts are available) and change them very slowly (if ever). Unsuccessful people make decisions very slowly and change them often and quickly.' After we hung up the phone, we were filled with a newfound sense of excitement, anxiety and wonder. We were excited about the new venture, anxious about the payment process, and were left wondering about how we would become masters at touching people's lives the way Bob Proctor has been for half a century.

It's been 90 days since that phone conversation, and we have successfully completed our payments, increased our income by a factor of 5, and have changed the lives of so many people around the world. This new shift in our lives took place because we let it take place. We were able to create a space facilitating the manifestation of these new ideas and results because we made a decision to do so. Ralph Waldo Emerson said, "Once a decision is made, the universe conspires to make it happen." This statement has been proven true over and over again in our lives, and we live by it every single day.

# How to Make a 'Successful' Decision

Decision making is an art that anyone can master and is a requirement if one wants to move forward towards a goal. This is the starting point of every journey. Imagine you are standing at the start of a dirt road, at the end of which your house is located. The reason you are standing on that road is because you decided that you wanted to go home. That decision brought you to a path that will eventually lead you to your destination.

Effective decision-making is an ability that very few people have mastered. Schools don't teach us how to properly make decisions, that's why even the smartest graduates cannot confidently decide to take advantage of an opportunity that will lead to success. On the other hand, we've got people without any formal education who can make important decisions that take them away from the masses and push them towards success.

When we feel confused about a decision, we get opposing thoughts and feelings running through our minds. This causes a state of disintegration because there is no order; in fact, there is only fear and anxiety, which ultimately lead to negative results. Napoleon Bonaparte, the French Emperor following the French Revolution, said, 'if there's no order, there is chaos.' Therefore, when we lack the ability to make quick and confident decisions, we put ourselves into a chaotic state of mind.

We've come to realize that indecision is a result of a lack of confidence and a self-image issue. Successful people make decisions in a confident manner, because they are not afraid of whether or not they made the right decision. There is no fear of failure; this is the key to being a strong decision maker. Lack of confidence (and the absence of certainty) arises from allowing our resources and environment to play a role in our decisions. We need to understand that we will never know how things are going to unfold until we make that ultimate decision. A teenager who has decided to acquire a driver's license will then figure out the process and learn how to drive and pass the test. A woman who has decided to bake an apple pie will then look for the recipe. The story unfolds after the decision is made. A decision provides a structure in which future events take place which are in harmony with that decision. You can only figure out which medical school to go to after deciding to become a doctor. You create a moneymaking business only after deciding that you want to be rich.

When an opportunity arises, think about your goal and what you want. Venture into a quiet and peaceful area and allow yourself to resonate with your gut feelings; don't talk to anyone, don't ask anyone. Don't be afraid of failure or what will result from your decision - this will allow you to avoid interference from your environment. The strongest and most successful people today make decisions quickly and change them very slowly, if ever. Practice making sound decisions and you will begin to attract the opportunities and ideas that will enable you to turn your burning desires into physical reality.

# Advanced Decision Making

When you're getting ready to host a dinner party, the first thing you do is make reservations; you reserve a table, you reserve a caterer and you reserve the entertainment for the night. You make sure to do this before anything else so you don't have to worry about problems occurring when your party begins. This is the essence of advanced decision-making; you make a commitment to something and you follow through no matter what the circumstances.

Imagine what you could accomplish by making decisions in advance for other areas of your life. Let's go back to Henry Ford, founder of the Ford Motor Company. Before establishing his company, Ford was taken on as chief engineer of the Edison Illuminating Company in 1893. This company was run by none other than Thomas Edison, a man who was ridiculed for his attempt and vision to invent incandescent light. While working for Edison, Ford kept developing his vision and ideas, and continued to work on his dream to invent a horseless carriage. In 1896, he created his first model: The Ford Quadricycle, and presented his automobile plans to Edison and his team of executives. As a man who believed in the impossible, Edison encouraged Ford to build a second, better model. Ford did so and introduced the Model T in 1908, after which the company posted 100% gains for the next few years. By the 1930's a wave of fear and downturns in the economy hit the United States, an era known today as The Great Depression. With the rise of Chevrolet, Ford knew he had to take it to another level, something that beat Chevrolet's six cylinder engines. Ford gave his engineers the 'impossible' task of inventing his world-renowned V-8 engine. Despite concerns and pleadings of helplessness from his staff, he pushed them forward and told them to 'produce it anyway.' A year went by without progress, but Ford was determined, and just like that something clicked - the Henry Ford V-8 engine was born.

Henry Ford's story is the perfect example of someone who makes decisions in advance; Ford didn't know how he was going to accomplish what the world viewed as 'impossible', he simply made an advanced decision that allowed him to plough through any issues and overcome any limitations. Neither his circumstances, the economy, nor the lack of resources prevented him from straying from his decision. So here's the ultimate key to decision-making: Start right here, right where you are, with whatever you've got.

PART II:

# A Power That
# Molds and Makes

CHAPTER 5

# The Roots Determine
# How The Tree Grows

There once was a farmer who lived in a small cottage with his wife. He was the most well-known farmer in his village, because he had a very special connection to nature. Everyone referred to him as 'the man with the green thumb.' Anything this man put into the soil, would bloom and blossom with bursts of color and freshness. No matter how hard other farmers tried, they couldn't match his results. His secret was that he selected only the best of the best seeds to plant in his rich soil; he refused to use anything that was less than perfect. He knew that if the seed was good, the plant itself would bloom beautifully.

We don't realize it, but we are tending to a garden everyday - the garden of our subconscious mind. You see, when we place thoughts or information into our minds, it goes through a gatekeeper, much like when a farmer guards his fields against bothersome crows and insects. Our gatekeeper in this case is called the conscious mind. Our conscious mind is our reasoning mind; it's the part of us that ties all the numbers together, weighs pros and cons, inputs all the logical points of a decision and spits out an answer.

No matter what we do, every single piece of information is going to pass through our conscious mind - but it's up to us to decide whether or not we want to allow that piece of information to open the gate and enter our subconscious mind. Every human being has 100% control over the information that passes through those doors; but we don't always EXERCISE this control, and over time we forget that we even have that control.

As we face positive and negative situations, we feed more and more declarations to our conscious mind, and we get so emotionally invested in them that we immediately open that gate. The garden in our subconscious mind picks up everything that comes through those doors, and we begin behaving and taking actions as if those declarations are true.

## Paradigms

When we were born, we didn't have a conscious mind; everything in our environment entered our subconscious mind, and our parents and environment began programming us based on that information. We did things unknowingly and without fear when we were kids, because we didn't have a conscious mind to help us differentiate between 'right' and 'wrong'. After the first few years, our conscious mind began to form and we started thinking for ourselves; but by this time, the programming was pretty well set.

If you really look at what our body is made of, we are simply a molecular structure moving at a very high speed of vibration. The thoughts that we think determine what vibration our body is in. You see, there is a power that is flowing to and through you. When this power is flowing to you, it just 'is' - you make it what it is. As this power flows through our conscious mind, we think thoughts and build ideas. However, these thoughts are only going to be in harmony with our programming. We've all got a multitude of habits and ideas that have been fixed into our subconscious mind over the years - that's what we call a paradigm. If your paradigm is set to believe that 'money is hard to earn,' you will *think* like a person who believes that money is hard to earn. This thought sets up a certain vibration in your body, which leads to the actions you take, and ultimately the result you get is based on those actions.

**Naveed:** *"I was raised to believe that money wasn't easy to earn, and I would constantly hear the phrase, 'money doesn't grow on trees.' My dad was the sole financer of our family, so as a kid I used to run to him, asking him to buy me a new toy. He would jokingly tell me, 'Where am I going to get the money?' or 'Why is everything you want so expensive?' These ideas were constantly lodged into my head,* *so eventually I stopped asking. As I got older, I began to look for a way to earn money the same way 96% of the population earns their income: I began to look for a job. I barely made enough to cover my needs, but I kept at it, because that's all I knew how to do. As I got married and settled down, my mind began frantically thinking of different ways I could increase my income. I thought of all the people who have made it big and I wondered what I was doing wrong. As I began to study, my wife and I eventually got involved with a lot of programs: T. Harv Eker's Millionaire Mind Intensive, Bob Proctor's Thinking Into Results program, as well as the Landmark Forum. After emerging with newfound knowledge and a different outlook, I reflected back on the way I used to look at money, and I couldn't believe the difference. The sole reason I wasn't earning money was because I believed that it was hard! All I needed to do was think like a person earning millions of dollars, and the ideas I needed to make that happen would flow to me. I began to work on changing this belief into one which was more empowering, and six months later I was earning money like it was the easiest thing in the world. Today, I can lay my life on the line when I say that we become what we think about.*

## What You Don't Fix, Your Kids Will Inherit

Think back to the number of times your son or daughter ran up to you and asked for something he/she wanted, and you said 'where are you going to get the money for that?' Children don't really hold onto things, so they let it go. The second time around they run up to you and ask for something else, and you say, 'Well how are you going to do that?' As these thoughts are constantly engrained into the child's mind, he/she is being programmed. They grow up to believe that unless they know *how* to do something, they have to let that dream go. Unless they have the money in their hands, they can't accomplish their dreams. They live their lives with this same worldview and then pass it on to their own children, and this cycle continues, over and over and over again. Instead of stopping your child with the *How*, tell them to figure it out! Tell them it's possible, and ask them to think of ideas of how to earn money. Allow them to develop their imagination and use their limitless potential to build a life that they will grow up to love. Your kids will grow up and accomplish things that will leave people around them in complete awe, and they will do so because you've planted a different seed in their minds, as compared to those of other children.

**Sonika:** *A small example of what children can accomplish can be demonstrated by the learning process of language. I grew up in an Indian family, born and raised in Bangkok, Thailand. I was surrounded by my grandmother who spoke Hindi, parents who spoke English and maids who spoke Thai. Naturally, I grew up knowing how to speak all three languages, because they were introduced to me before I had the conscious ability to say, 'I can't learn this.' By the time I was attending university in San Francisco, people were absolutely amazed that I could speak three different languages, and this amazed me in return because I thought it was so normal! Everyone I knew back home could speak so many different languages so we grew up believing this was a normal part of life; but to those who lived in Western countries it was an amazing accomplishment. It is absolutely imperative to start your kids early with beliefs that will allow them to separate themselves from the masses and use their imaginations to build an absolutely beautiful life. Remember, what you don't fix, your kids will inherit.*

## How to Change Your Paradigm

Paradigms don't want to be changed. Think of how hard it is to change any habit or belief. When you're getting ready for work in the morning, which foot do you pull the sock over first? Do you start by putting your right leg into your pants or your left leg? You've probably never thought about this because **it's all automatic!** We move in complete automation! Your habits and ideas are programmed into you like a computer, and you've lived with them all these years as if there were no other way to do things. Do you know that majority of people who graduate with honors are completely broke? Do you know that a lot of successful people today had little to no formal education? Yet they're earning millions of dollars a year. The belief that you need to have a formal education or business experience to be successful is absolutely **not true.** It is not true. This is just a small example of the hundreds of ideas and beliefs we have stuck in our mind.

Imagine that you believe that losing weight is hard. You get so emotionally involved in this belief, that you open the gate to your subconscious mind, and it gets planted as a seed in your mind. As you repeatedly think that 'losing weight is hard,' it begins to take root in your mind as being irrefutable. Can you imagine how strong that belief would be after ten years? Can you imagine the actions you would have to take because of that belief? Can you guess what your results would be? After allowing that thought to take root, your body goes straight into that vibration, and begins to control your actions. With the same thoughts repeating in your mind, how can you expect a different result? This right here is what we call 'getting stuck in a rut.'

Our paradigm was created due to repetition of information being constantly impressed into our subconscious mind. The positive information blossomed into beautiful flowers, giving us absolutely amazing results, while the negative information took root and built up a field of weeds in our subconscious mind. Unfortunately, for the majority of people today, their subconscious garden is filled with more weeds than flowers. Aristotle once said, 'educating the mind without educating the heart is no education at all.' When we think of the heart, we think of the organ that pumps blood throughout our bodies. Our heart is actually our subconscious mind; it's the emotional mind, the part that actually controls our behavior by regulating the vibration in our body. Now, our paradigm doesn't just control our actions, it also controls our logic (since it controls our whole belief system). If these ideas were placed into our minds through repetition, it only makes sense that we would get rid of these ideas with the same process of repetition, also called autosuggestion. Every idea is initially deemed illogical - Thomas Edison's light bulb, Henry Ford's horseless carriage, the Wright Brother's airplane - the list goes on and on. Look around your home today; how logical is a light bulb? How logical is it to travel internationally on an airplane? We can't live without these inventions, and they make complete sense in today's world, but they sure didn't at first. Napoleon Hill wrote an entire chapter on autosuggestion in his book *Think and Grow Rich*. He said, 'Like the wind that carries one ship east and another west, the law of autosuggestion will lift you up or pull you down according to the way you set your sails of thought.' Your subconscious mind has no idea how to differentiate fact from fiction. So it depends entirely on what you choose to believe and plant in that garden. It is absolutely illogical to repeat something to yourself 100 times a day. It is illogical to read the same book over and over again, but it has to be done because that's how our old paradigm was conceived. We have to replace our old paradigm with a new one - eventually, the old belief will die from lack of nourishment and the new one will take root and start to control you. After 50 years of research, this is one of the two known ways to change a paradigm. The other way is one we cannot control. It is done by experiencing an emotional impact, something that changes your entire world. Emotional impacts are usually negative, and we have no idea on how to determine when they are going to occur. So the only way we can change our paradigms on purpose is by repeating what we want until the things that we don't want begin to disappear.

# CHAPTER 6

# A Glass Jug

It's pretty amazing how we live our lives and go through our daily routine without thinking about what we have to do. We drive our car a certain way, we put our clothes on in a certain way, and we even have a routine when we wake up in the morning; we are habitual beings and all our habits are dictated by our paradigm. There is one idea in our paradigm that we rarely think about, yet it controls our behavior in the same way an airplane automatically navigates its way back on course after it goes off track. This part of our paradigm is our self-image, an idea discovered in the 1960s by Dr. Maxwell Maltz. Dr. Maltz was a cosmetic surgeon and the author of a book called 'Psycho Cybernetics.' 'Psyche,' in Greek, means 'mind,' and 'cybernetics' is known as the science of control and communication in animals and machines. Dr. Maltz discovered that one of his patients began behaving like a different person once his outer appearance changed - the patient acted more confidently. However, another patient continued to experience self-esteem issues regardless of any change in appearance. At this very moment, Dr. Maltz discovered that we hold two images in our mind: one image is what we project out to the world, while the other image is how we see ourselves on the screen of our minds. This self-image literally determines what we bring into our lives and how we deal with each situation.

When we were born, our environment and the people around us shaped and stored information into our subconscious - information that helped form ideas, ultimately coming together to create our self-image. If a child was constantly acknowledged and complimented, he or she would grow up to be comfortable with him or herself and be a top performer in any field. If they were always told off, discouraged, or bullied, they would grow up to be insecure and frustrated.

Have you noticed that whenever you begin your journey towards any goal, if you aren't fully invested in achieving it, you end up getting bored, quitting or failing? Why does this happen? It happens because our body is a cybernetic mechanism which brings us 'back on course' when we break our comfort zone. This is the reason so many people quit: they do something for a while, they start seeing results, they get comfortable and then they get stuck. If a child has a self-image that he or she is a student who gets poor grades in school, the results will reflect that perception. Yet you will see parents and teachers finding all sorts of ways to get the child 'back on track' by taking away their toys or rewarding them with a gift if they do well. In that situation, the child will improve and get better grades, but their cybernetic mechanism will eventually bring them back on track to getting poor grades again. It is the image they hold in their mind that determines their grades. If we understand the root cause of these results, we can learn to truly be in control.

**Naveed:** *"I would like to take you on a journey back through time and space when I was just a teenager. Many of you know what kids go through at that age; they are confused about whom they are but they are also excited to have new experiences. Now if you were a chubby little boy like me, you would remember the amount of teasing and bullying received from friends and class mates. There was a point in my life that I had become extremely self-conscious about my appearance, until I even convinced myself that this was simply 'who I am,' and that I couldn't get along with most of the guys because of their interest in sports (which at that time I had absolutely no interest in whatsoever).*

*There was a turning point that came around sophomore year in high school. I felt a compulsion to join the reserved officer military training for 3 years while completing the last remaining years of high school. According to the rules in Thailand, I was required to complete this training before turning 18; otherwise I would have to test my luck by picking red or black chits out of a box, which would determine whether or not I would have to join the army for 2 years. I wanted to just take the training and get it over with because I knew I had to simply attend 4 hours of class every Saturday for 6 months each year. Now, that seemed a lot more appealing to me than joining the military for 2 years away from home.*

*Unfortunately, I discovered there was a drastic test that I had to pass if I wanted to make it. I began to lose hope in having any chance at all of taking this route. I felt lost and depressed when I heard about the requirements of the test because at the time I could barely run further than 100 meters without getting exhausted, or do more than 10 pushups at a time. The test required me to sprint 800 meters in less than 3 minutes, perform 55 military pushups, and 35 sit ups. I went back home from school, completely dejected, where my dad saw me staring off into space thinking about the situation. He came into the room, closing the door behind him, and asked me what had happened. I told him that I had to pass a rigorous test in order to enter the training, and how I was unable to do even one fourth of the requirements. My dad then put his arms around me and told me something I have never forgotten: 'you can't predetermine if you've passed or failed, your job is to do your best.' Having been in the Navy as a young boy himself, my dad promised to train me and get me fit enough to past the test. The next day he woke me up at 6 A.M. to go run in the park - an extremely dreadful experience. I was taking breaks every 100 meters of jogging for 10 minutes at a time. Then as I kept pushing myself every day to get better at building my endurance and muscle strength in my arms and abdomen, I eventually got fit enough to pass the test - and I did just that.*

*At that moment I decided that I wanted to become slim and fit for the sake of having good health. Soon enough I realized something strange, yet so common. I would begin a workout routine and do well for a little while, but 3 months later I would get lazy and consume junk food (which I knew would lead me to gain everything back). This was a constant roller coaster for me. I couldn't figure out why it was happening because I whole-heartedly wanted to be consistent. Eventually I joined a fitness gym a few blocks away from my house and I began searching for a role model online. After I found one, I kept imagining that I had a physique like that person; I even acted as if I was fit by throwing in dialogues to people of how I have amazing abs. Ever since then, I remained consistent in maintaining a healthy weight.*

*After studying and understanding self-image, it is absolutely clear that when I was younger I had created a self-image about myself that I was 'fat and chubby' based on what the outside world had told me. That self-image had remained in my mind even when I joined the military training, and it became clear why I kept eating junk and slacking off. In other words, I was programmed to gain back the weight every time I would lose it because my mind was fixed with a certain image. When I continuously saw myself as a fit person with 6-pack abs, my self-image changed and my body conformed to that new idea I had about myself. I had changed my paradigm and I didn't even know it.*

Self-Image is such a simple concept and yet so powerful if it is understood correctly. But if misunderstood, it will lead to results we don't want over and over again. Since the majority of the population has been taught to conform to society, most of us remain stuck within our own limitations. Our self-image works just like a thermostat that functions a certain way, and our physical body simply follows that mechanism. Earl Nightingale wrote a concrete story called 'A Pumpkin In A Jug.' In the story, he talks about a farmer who grew pumpkins in his farm and one day, out of curiosity, he poked a pumpkin seed into a jug and forgot about it. At harvest season, he saw that his farm was filled with giant pumpkins; however, there was that one seed that didn't look quite right. The seed in the jug had grown into the shape of the jug - no more, no less. The farmer was completely baffled by his experiment because he realized that the pumpkin grew large enough until it hit its limit and stopped growing. The farmer kept his piece of experiment as a show case for satisfaction. His son, who was an assistant professor of psychology at the university, wanted to take the jug to his school and use it as a teaching tool about psychological limitations.

Our belief and self-image, like the jug, determines the shape and size we grow into. The question that needs to be asked is who determines our limits and barriers? We can have absolutely no limits whatsoever if we wanted, which would give us the freedom to tap into the infinite power and potential that lies dormant within us. We are the only creatures on the planet that can determine how far we want to grow - that's why we are truly born free. Bob Proctor always says, 'the only limits in our life are those we impose on ourselves.'

# How To Change Your Self-Image

The story about the pumpkin in the jar is one of the best stories that could ever have been told with respect to understanding what self-image really is. The jug is to the pumpkin what limitation is to man. If we sit quietly in a room somewhere, get into a completely relaxed state of mind and attempt to listen to the dialogue we are having with and about ourselves in our minds, it will become very evident what kind of image we hold about ourselves. There is an infinite power that animates and penetrates the cosmos, and that power also flows to and through us, ultimately leading to the thoughts we create. The only thoughts we will ever have are going to be in exact harmony with the self-image we hold of ourselves.

There is one amazing exercise you can do in order to help you understand your own self-image, and eventually change it into what you want it to be. You need to write a script about yourself. Not your situation, not the story of your past, just YOU. Who would you like to be? Begin jotting down ideas of the person you would like to be, and read it over and over again. Allow yourself to totally relax and feel like you are already that person and you will begin to see those results manifesting in no time. Start becoming the person you aspire to be and start living that way. There is a great book called 'The Art of Acting' which is essentially a compilation of Stella Adler's teachings. Stella Adler taught actors to walk, talk and live the character they were going to play. Actors imagine themselves to be someone else all the time; in fact, they're pros at it! So if actors are studying the character they are trying to play in a movie, we should study the person we are aspiring to be in our own lives! Study your dream, really think about every aspect of who you want to be, and then begin creating a plan and taking action to manifest each of those qualities. Break down those comfort zones and allow your cybernetic mechanism to acquire a new optimal state of being. Make success your norm, and you'll be on your way to creating bigger and better fantasies.

CHAPTER 7

# Your Invisibility Cloak

**S**onika: *"I recently came across a book that had been locked away for years, one that had just been released to the public in 2014. It was 'Outwitting The Devil' by Napoleon Hill, and the entire book is a conversation between Napoleon Hill and the Devil. Now did Hill really sit down in his living room and have a chat with a red monster with horns and a sharp tail? Not exactly. Every cell in our body has a positive and negative charge. When we are thinking positive thoughts, and we impress them onto our emotional mind, our entire body goes into a positive charge, or a positive vibration. It's exactly the same scenario when we entertain negative thoughts. According to Hill, the Devil basks in the negative pole of our body, and to take control of the mind the Devil uses his number one favorite tool: fear. I was astounded at this information, but at the same time it made so much sense! When we entertain negative thoughts or emotions we aren't in control of ourselves, because we can't think or take action clearly when we are angry or afraid. I can't even keep count of the number of times I have caused damage to my relationships, and myself, simply because I didn't have control. If Hill was right about anything, it was the fact that people fear two things the most in this world: death and poverty.*

*I was brought up by parents who are rock-solid believers in spirituality. I believe in it too, but the thought of not having control over my destiny (which is what my parents believed) didn't sit well with me. I would always feel like any effort I put in to achieve my goals would be nullified by the belief that 'it was meant to be.' So I grew up to be someone who loved looking for all the answers: ghosts, spirits, and near-death experiences, I wanted to know everything. One day, my husband and I came across an interview by Anita Moorjani. At this point, I was already successfully coaching clients through Bob Proctor's amazing 'Thinking Into Results' program, one that really allowed me to believe in spirituality in a free and powerful way. So when I heard of Anita Moorjani's breathtaking experience in the after-life, I was thoroughly convinced that the material I have dedicated my life to is 100% real. I couldn't wait to share this material with everyone around me.*

*The following story is based on the original NDE (Near Death Experience) description that Anita Moorjani submitted to the Near Death Research Foundation in August 2006: Anita Moorjani was diagnosed with Hodgkin's Lymphoma, a type of cancer that affects the body's lymphatic system and deteriorates the body's immune system. Told that she was at the end of the road, on February 2nd, 2006 Anita was rushed to the hospital, as she slipped into a coma. The doctors prepared her husband for her death, assuring him they would do their best but her survival was unlikely. At this point, Anita was experiencing something incredible - she was able to hear conversations between her doctor and her husband that were taking place 40 feet away. She then 'crossed over' to another dimension, where she was instantly engulfed by a feeling of pure love. She realized how much power and potential we humans truly possess, and she came to realize exactly why she got cancer. She had been suppressing her desires all her life, trying to please those around her. She had a choice in that moment, to choose between life and death. She decided she had a purpose to fulfill, for her family as well as for people all around the world. As she drifted back into her body, her organs began to function, and within days, her body was almost cancer-free. Anita Moorjani has been cancer-free ever since. Listening to Anita Moorjani's story was a validation that I was on the right track.*

Everything in life begins with understanding. When we understand how a plane works, we are not afraid when we hit turbulence. When we understand how electricity works, we don't become frantic with fear when the lights go out. Everything - absolutely everything - begins with understanding, and it's no different when it comes to understanding how our minds work.

As discussed earlier in this book, we all have a conscious mind, a subconscious mind, and a body. Our conscious mind is where we form thoughts. Our subconscious mind is made up of a paradigm, including all our habits, beliefs and our self-image. Our body is simply an instrument of the mind, because the mind is movement; it's in every cell of the body. When we proceed through life with ignorance, and we are unwilling to learn and grow, we fill our conscious mind with worry and doubt - simply because we haven't taken action to increase our awareness. As worry and doubt become a habit, we impress this energy onto our subconscious mind, which eventually turns into fear. Because the body is the instrument of the mind, it expresses this fearful vibration into every cell, ultimately manifesting in our body as anxiety. Now people don't express anxiety, they suppress it. This suppression leads to depression, depression leads to disease, and disease ultimately leads to disintegration of our body. 1% of the population is earning 96% of all money being earned through multiple sources. Another 1% of the population invests money for money. Interestingly enough, in Napoleon Hill's conversation with the Devil, the latter confessed that he currently has control of over 98% of the population through the use of his favorite tool: fear. So it's safe to assume that 98% of the population is completely unaware of this information, and continue to live life with worry, doubt and fear. Now looking at the opposite end of the spectrum, when we truly understand who we are and how our minds work, we are able to break through our fears and achieve amazing results. Make no mistake, successful people are not free of fear; in fact, they experience it more so than the rest of the population as they are taking bigger risks. Fear is a word we use to describe the conflicting vibrations that occur when we are presented with a new, uncomfortable situation. However, due to the fact that they understand the human mind and the true power and potential we possess, they are able to embrace fear and move ahead at the same time. So when we study and increase our knowledge, understanding develops in our conscious mind. This understanding leads to faith on a subconscious level. When we have faith based on *understanding* as opposed to *blind* faith, we very rarely return to our old ways because we understand *why* we have faith. By having faith, we allow ourselves to experience a state of well-being. When we feel great, we become more expressive, which ultimately leads to acceleration (we pick up speed due to confidence). We are calm and at-ease; this puts us in a creative state through which we can provide greater service and build bigger and better fantasies.

## How To Permanently Remove Your Invisibility Cloak

For those who have a problem with expressing themselves, it's hard to believe in what has been presented thus far. Since acceptance of fear requires faith based on understanding, keep reading to figure out where these theories came from.

Remember when we said that we are nothing but a set of molecules in a very high speed of vibration? We are nothing but energy, and we've got energy flowing to and through us. Now if we examine the only two sources of education we've got access to (Science and Theology), and we ask, '*what is energy?*' we're not going to get two different answers. Science will tell you that energy just is; it always was and always has been, it's equally present in all places at the same time, and it can never be created or destroyed. Theologians will give you the exact same answer. So if we really think about it, if energy is equally present at all places at the same time, and we have the same energy flowing to and through us, why are some people winning while others are not? It's simple: the ones who aren't winning are not aware of this information. You've got the same energy flowing into you that Thomas Edison had. You've got the same energy flowing into you that Steve Jobs had. Yet, people say they don't have any energy. All these great men didn't agree on a whole lot, but they did agree on one thing: man becomes what he thinks about.

As this information trickled down through generations, it ended up in the hands of Andrew Carnegie, a man who knew absolutely nothing about the steel business, but was able to become the richest man in the world at one point. Andrew Carnegie mentored Napoleon Hill, who in turn mentored Earl Nightingale. Earl Nightingale was Bob Proctor's mentor, and through working with Bob, we are able to share this information with you.

Now we have a conscious mind, and we can accept or reject thoughts. When energy flows into our consciousness, it's exactly the same as the energy flowing into your neighbor. Based on our paradigm we turn that energy into thoughts, thoughts that are in harmony with our conditioning. That's why employees who go through the exact same training come out of it with different results. Students sitting in the exact same classroom with the exact same teacher graduate with different transcripts.

**Naveed:** "*I remember a night when I stayed over at my in-law's place; their house was in a small neighborhood, mostly quiet and peaceful. One night, there was a blackout, and as if it was routine, my wife got up and went outside to the balcony. She started looking at other houses to see if it was just our house that had problems or whether it was everyone in the neighborhood. It became apparent that only our house was affected. We waited for a few minutes until the lights came back on, but I noticed that only 10% of the bulbs in the chandelier above her were working. I was faced with the realization that if even some of the bulbs are working, there's nothing* *wrong with the electricity - there's something wrong with the bulb. It's exactly the same when it comes to us; we've got all the power we need; we just need to turn it into what we want!*

The energy flowing into you is exactly like electricity is to a light bulb. When we've got a problem with a light bulb, we know that we aren't short of electricity (unless we haven't paid our bills). We'll try to figure out what to do, we'll replace it, and we'll check the plug socket. We'll do everything to get that bulb to turn on, and eventually we figure it out. So when you've got energy flowing to you, if you want bigger results, plug in a bigger idea! Start thinking like a person who is successful, and you'll open up the space for more electricity to flow in and eventually manifest that success.

Make a decision that from now on, you're going to have full power over what you allow to flow into your conscious mind. You're going to reject what you don't want and accept what you want. Aristotle once said 'It is the mark of an educated mind to entertain a thought without accepting it.' The ability to choose between thoughts comes from our ability to reason. Reason is one of our higher faculties, it allows thinking. Without power flowing into our consciousness, we would have no energy from which we could build thoughts. When we combine a number of different thoughts together, we build ideas; those ideas are then introduced to us over and over until they become locked in our subconscious. That's where fear begins. A lot of people are afraid of flying, but if news channels told us about those thousands of flights daily that actually made it safely to their destination, would people still be afraid of flying? Probably not. Everything begins with knowledge and our level of awareness.

We are God's highest form of creation, and our mind is what separates us from the animal kingdom. Archibald MacLeish once said, 'The only thing about man that is man is his mind. Everything else you can find in a pig or a horse.' If you watch an animal in its natural habitat, it is evident the animal is comfortable. If you take an animal out of its natural environment, and place it in downtown New York, the animal becomes disoriented. We are the only creatures on this planet that have the ability to create our own environment, yet we are completely disoriented all of the time. Take an acorn for instance; the spiritual DNA of an acorn is absolutely perfect (just like every other living creature). When an acorn is planted in the soil and given the right nourishment, it flourishes and expresses its natural perfection, turning itself from that small seed into a big, tall oak tree. However, if you take an acorn out of its natural environment, it doesn't grow - in fact it disintegrates. The plant and animal kingdoms operate solely on instinct, so when they are in their natural habitat, they are the best they can be. It's an all or nothing game. Human beings have an amazing asset: our minds. We have the ability to create our own environment, so we can flourish in almost any situation! So few of us actually use this ability to create the world we want.

The news may be right about the stock market crash, and your parents may be right about the fact that you're not confident enough to run a business - but these things don't have to be true for you! You can reject these ideas and believe what you wish, because those beliefs will eventually manifest into your results. The next time you're afraid of something, learn more about it. Lift off that invisibility cloak, find your voice, and choose your thoughts wisely.

# CHAPTER 8

# Falling In Love
# With Fear

**S**onika: *"I've always loved the idea of the unknown; digging deeper and exploring places others have never been to, just to discover the truth. That's probably the reason I'm crazy about ghosts, Halloween and outer space. My parents refuse to go watch a horror movie because they believe it has a negative effect on the mind, but I refused to let it bother me. I was just obsessed with the idea of where we go after we die and why hauntings occur. I loved every bit of the fear I felt when I was entering a haunted house at a theme park. I remember sitting in my room alone at 2 A.M. with the lights off watching Ghost Adventures for the first time. The fear didn't bother me because I was expanding my knowledge of why these phenomena exist. I realized that if you fall in love with something, and you love the process of learning more about it, the fear that comes along with it would have little effect on you.*

We as humans, along with everything else in this universe, operate with the Law of Opposites. We've got hot and cold, up and down, inside and outside. One cannot exist without the other, yet they cannot exist in the same place at the same time. It's an interesting paradox to think about. If we love someone, automatically the things we don't like about them slowly start to disappear as we keep focusing on the parts we love. Similarly, when we experience fear, there is always an opposite side to the situation. Kyle Cease, a comedian in the personal development industry once said, 'If you don't like something, fall in love with it.' This makes complete sense, because when you fall in love with something you fear, that very fear cannot sustain itself (or it will be reduced by a large degree).

According to Darwin's theory of Evolution, we evolved into humans from other creatures that occupy this planet, and if you dig really deep, you will come to realize that we still possess some of their characteristics. One very apparent quality that animals and humans have in common is our body's ability to go into 'fight or flight mode.' Fight or flight mode is our body's way of telling us that we have come across something we've never faced before. It's an animalistic instinct that we possess.

Think back to a time when someone said something to you, or maybe you did something you weren't supposed to and you were confronted about it. You were angry, you were afraid; you didn't know whether to move forward and fight for yourself, or to run and hide in a hole. You had shivers going down your spine. That's your body going into fight or flight mode. It's no different when we're faced with a life-changing decision about money, relationships, health or any other opportunity we come across. We really want to go for it, but we run smack into a wall of: 'Should I do this?' We decide we don't have the time or money for the opportunity and we let it go. We return to our comfort zone where we feel safe, and we talk ourselves into believing that we're okay where we are.

In the previous chapter, we spoke a bit about how our level of awareness dictates our actions and our results. When we finish high school, we decide to increase our knowledge about a certain subject, and we go off to college. After graduation we may continue to take another course, or we go ahead and get a job in the industry we majored in. Now here's where most people go wrong: *they stop learning.* T. Harv Eker said something absolutely brilliant regarding to education: 'Rich people always learn and grow. Poor people think they already know.' This is absolutely brilliant, because our level of awareness is a major indicator when it comes to determining our level of success.

You see, when you expand your level of awareness, you automatically enter a new realm of possibilities.

Take a second to get a piece of paper and pen. Now draw a tiny dot in the middle of the paper. This tiny dot represents your level of awareness. Everything you've got in life - relationships, money, etc. - is an expression of your own level of awareness. People suffering from headaches are not suffering from headaches because they want to - they're suffering from headaches because they are not aware of how to eliminate them. It's their head; they made it ache and they can make it stop. Now draw a bigger dot over the first one. If that tiny dot were responsible for all the results in your life, imagine how your life would change if you could magnify your level of awareness by that small amount? You'd earn more money, your relationships would be better, and you'd live in a healthier body. Now draw an even bigger dot on that paper. It's absolutely limitless because this universe is limitless!

When we're faced with fear or a situation that we don't know what to do with, that's where we lack the awareness about how to move forward. The more you know about something, the less afraid of it you'll be. Bob Proctor told us a story once, about being on a plane during turbulence. He was holding on tight and there was fear because he didn't understand what was going on. He saw a man sitting absolutely calm in this whole chaotic situation, and he approached him, wondering why he wasn't afraid. The man laughed and said, 'Well I train people to fly these things.' Bob then asked him why planes don't just fall out of the sky. The man said, 'You can make a rock fly if you've got enough thrust behind it.' Think about that for a minute. We never think of something 'flying' if we just pick it up and throw it. But that's technically what it does. If you pick up a rock and throw it with enough force, it will fly for a certain amount of time, lose its thrust power, and fall back down. Bob has never been afraid of flying since that incident.

It only takes an increase in awareness about something in order to stop being afraid of it. So it makes sense that if we want to stop letting fear control our decisions, we need to be aware of why we have fear in the first place. Can you imagine laying out all the pieces of a puzzle on a tabletop, only to realize you're missing the lid of the box that has the image on it? How would you know what pieces go together? How would you know what you're creating? That is exactly the problem that we have when it comes to understanding who we are. Make no mistake, if you want to change the results in your life, you must first understand the creator of those results: your mind.

In 1934, Dr. Thurman Fleet realized that doctors were treating symptoms of disease instead of the root cause which was forcing the patients to contract the disease over and over again. He decided that because no one has ever seen the mind, they were unaware of how to change it. So Dr. Thurman Fleet proceeded to create an image of the mind to bring order and understanding to people all over the world. We have introduced this very picture to our clients and the results are absolutely mind-blowing. According to Bob, once you raise your conscious awareness, you can never lose it. That is where the idea that 'You can't go back' really comes from. You don't lose the awareness that you develop. When you learn to ride a bike or drive a car, you never really forget how to do it once it's formulated into a habit.

## The 7 Levels of Awareness

Based on Bob Proctor's 50 years of research, we now know that we have 7 different levels of awareness. The first level is called Animal Instinct. This first level of awareness boils down to our most natural, animalistic instincts; this is where we go into fight or flight mode when confronted with an unknown, uncomfortable situation.

Imagine that you cheated on a test, and you were hoping no one would ever find out. One day, your teacher calls you into her office and tells you that she has something important to discuss. It has come to her attention that you were dishonest, and you cheated on your test. You can imagine the chaos going through your body at that exact moment. You're guilty and afraid, and you may also feel like you want to defend yourself. Physically, when we are in this chaotic mix of frequencies, we tend to shiver and shake. We don't know whether to fight and face the situation, or to just run away. When an animal is in a vulnerable situation, having come across a predator, it reacts in the exact same way. It remains still for a few moments, figuring out what to do; it is in fight or flight mode. Because of this animalistic instinct, we tend to *react* to situations instead of *respond* to them. A lot of the time, we don't even realize that we are in fight or flight mode, as it may not be as obvious as the scenario described previously. A new job offer, a new opportunity, buying a new house or any other situation that is outside of your comfort zone will cause your body to enter this animalistic state. Now, here's where we tend to run frantic; asking others for their opinions and stressing about what to do. Eventually we decide it's better to be safe than sorry, and back we go, straight into our comfort zone.

Our second level of awareness is called 'Following the Masses.' You've surpassed your animalistic instincts and have moved toward seeking guidance on making a decision. We've been conditioned since the day we were born to follow the crowd. We've been taught to conform to society because, according to our conditioning, we can never go wrong by doing so. Now as we discussed earlier, 1% of the population earns 96% of all the money. A tiny 1%, the ones who successfully strayed away from the masses, is earning all the money. That's a big blow to our usual way of thinking, because we have been taught a different definition of success as compared to that 1%. Success lies in your way of thinking, and if you're conforming to your society and surroundings, you will produce results which are indistinguishable from those of the masses. It can be no other way.

This brings us to the third level of awareness, where you have the desire to do something greater. This level is called 'Aspiration,' as you're aspiring to be different, to be like the leaders in your industry. You've repeatedly followed the masses, you've been stuck in a rut for a long time, and now you're looking to play the bigger game. In this level of awareness, you have simply become aware of your desire, you now know what you really want, but you haven't acted on it. This desire is still in your conscious mind, and you are fiddling around with it. However, without action, this desire cannot lead you to the results that you desire.

The fourth level of awareness consists of 'Individualism.' You have started to express your uniqueness to the world, and you are starting to stand out from the masses. This level comes with opposition, as you are going against everything you've been taught, as well as the logic of those around you. Einstein once said, 'Great spirits have always encountered violent opposition from mediocre minds.' Up until this point, you are still stuck in YOU. In other words, you are still stuck in your old patterns, though you have become AWARE of these patterns, and your desire to change them.

Now the fifth level of awareness is where you begin to break free, but it is also the level where most people get stuck. This level of awareness is called 'Discipline.' You know what you want, you've expressed your wants and uniqueness to the world, and now you need to take action. You need to give yourself a command regarding what to do next, and you need to follow it through. Demand something of yourself that is going to empower you to keep moving forward; make a decision!

Robert Collier said, 'Success is the sum of small efforts repeated day in, day out.' Remember, when discipline disappears, your desire turns into a mere wish, and you get stuck. The biggest reason for failure at this level of awareness is that people are setting the wrong goals, and they don't know what their biggest desires and passions are. This eventually results in a lack of persistence. If you're not passionate about your goal, just like the airplane we spoke about earlier, you're going to lose your thrust power, and fall back down.

The Discipline level is where you've made a decision and given yourself a command. Now it's fairly obvious that you will face some setbacks, along with trials and errors. This brings us to our sixth level of awareness: 'Experience.' This where real learning takes place - you're taking a hands-on approach, accepting failure as a stepping stone and NOT a permanent location. At this level of awareness, you're allowing yourself to be open-minded, you're learning from your mistakes, and you're building new ideas.

# How to Fall in Love with Fear

If there's one thing successful people love, it's a challenge. They love to do new things, and get better at what they're doing. When you realize that being afraid simply means you've entered a new realm of possibilities, you're going to take advantage of this new experience and produce even bigger results. After figuring out what works for you, and setting up a proper study process, you will have gained enough experience to enter into the seventh and highest level of awareness: 'Mastery.' This is where the big league operators are; the leaders of your industry are all at this level. You are absolutely in love with what you do. You are as certain of yourself and your knowledge, as you are of the fact that if you pick up a pen and drop it, it's going to fall. You begin to respond to your outside circumstances instead of reacting to them, no one but you has control over your destiny.

Start thinking of someone you admire. What does that person do on a daily basis? What are their success habits? How much do they earn? What are their hobbies? Learning more about someone who has mastered the industry you wish to be a part of is absolutely imperative; because to acquire similar results we must adopt similar thoughts and habits. A person who's earning $50,000 a year is not earning $50,000 because they want to. They are earning $50,000 because they aren't aware of how to earn $100,000 a year! They are thinking the thoughts of a person who is earning $50,000 a year, so they will take action based on their thoughts, and as a result they will earn $50,000 year after year. Even if they start off slow in the first three months, they will end up with $50,000 by the end of the year. It's all programmed!

Let's say you are earning $100,000 a year in your business and your goal is to earn a million in a year's time. You have to raise your level of awareness of how to earn a million dollars a year, and you will start taking action based on your increase in awareness. Start changing your frequency, begin to walk, talk and feel like a person who is earning a million dollars a year. This will allow you to tap into the correct frequency, you will attract thoughts of a person earning a million dollars a year, and you'll increase your awareness on how to manifest those thoughts in your physical world through trial and error. Darryl Anka once said, 'Everything is energy and that's all there is to it. Match the frequency of the reality you want and you cannot help but get that reality. It can be no other way. This is not philosophy. This is physics.'

# CHAPTER 9

# Inside Conversations

**S**onika: *"I remember my mom used to tell me stories about her dreams, ones that could in some way give her an idea of what was going to happen in the near future. As we already know that we are conditioned genetically and environmentally, it didn't take me long to figure out I had a similar sense of intuition. One night, when I was 15, I remember I had a very rough time falling asleep; I couldn't figure out what was keeping me awake, as I knew I was tired. I could hear dogs howling in the distance and I just felt this sense of urgency in my chest. I lay wide-awake, staring up at my ceiling with a million thoughts shooting across my mind. I finally managed to fall asleep watching the sunrise at 6 A.M. Before I knew it, my maid was shaking me, whispering to me that my grandfather had passed away. It took me a few minutes to make sense of it, as he was in India at the time and I hadn't seen him for a few weeks. However, I didn't feel an ounce of sadness; in fact, I wasn't even shocked. I didn't know why, but I had a gut feeling all night that something was about to happen.*

*This intuitive experience took place yet again when my grandmother passed away just two years ago, but this time it was a lot stronger. During the time of my wedding my grandmother was in the hospital as she was diagnosed with bone cancer. She was in her last stages, so the wedding was a bittersweet moment for all of us. I left a week later to go on my honeymoon, and on the 7th night I was there, I experienced yet another sleepless night. We always had a mosquito and insect problem being in Bali, but on this particular night, the mosquitos were bothering me more than usual. I was feeling claustrophobic and I couldn't fall asleep no matter how hard I tried. When I finally began dozing off, I got a phone call from my mom at 4 A.M., telling me my grandmother had passed away. Yet again, I knew what she was going to say the second I heard my phone ring.*

NAVEED ASIF & SONIKA MADARASMI ASIF

*Because of these intuitive feelings, I've always been able to deal with the death of a loved one fairly easily, because I always had a hint that the situation was going to occur. But nothing prepared me for what took place afterwards. A week after I returned home from my honeymoon, I woke up one morning in complete shock, grappling for anybody I could talk to about what had just happened. I'm sure you've heard stories about loved ones visiting people in their dreams; some believe it's just a dream while others swear it was real. I knew it was 100% real, and even while writing these words I can remember every single detail of my conversation with my grandmother.*

*In the dream I was standing in my old room near my closet. My grandmother had already passed away and I was standing there, thinking about her for a few minutes. All of a sudden I felt a huge force push me through space and time. I felt a gush of wind and colors were just flying by. I couldn't breathe, I couldn't see and I didn't know what was happening. After what felt like ages, everything stopped. The wind died, my eyes began to adjust, and I was standing in pin-drop silence. I could see bright white light everywhere I looked. There were no walls, no floor; it was just pure white light. Then I saw her. My grandmother sitting in front of me (I didn't even notice whether there was a chair there or not), dressed in a pink Indian suit, the one she always used to wear on special occasions. I looked at her completely dumbfounded; I didn't even know what to say. What do you say to someone who has passed on? What do you ask them? What are they even allowed to tell you? When I finally found the courage to open my mouth, I realized we weren't communicating through spoken words. She already knew what I was thinking, and she asked me, 'How are you?' It seemed we were communicating telepathically, and my mind was picking up the energy and turning it into a language I understood. My grandmother never learned English so it made sense that we were communicating on a whole different level. I replied saying I was married. She said she knew, and she smiled. I couldn't think of what else to say, so I asked her where she was. She didn't reply; it's almost as if she wasn't allowed to. She then pulled out a piece of paper and began scribbling something on it. I looked over and saw the words 'English' and 'Train.' I asked her what she was doing, and she smirked, informing me that she was trying to learn English. I was overflowing with so many different emotions that all I could do was hug her and kiss her forehead. I started thinking about moments with her, and about my parents and my husband. All of a sudden, without any formal notice, I felt that gush of wind once again, only this time I was going backwards. Something inside me knew that because I was thinking of my attachments in the physical world, I was being pushed back there, because there is no place for those in the world after death.*

*I jerked awake, completely sweating and confused. I sat there in complete shock trying to make sense of what I just saw, but I couldn't shake the intense emotions I was feeling. I could still feel my grandmother's warmth, the feel of the cotton suit she*

56

*was wearing, and I knew that what I had just experienced was 100% real. It was her, she had come to visit me, and there was no doubt about it.*

You may or may not have experienced a dream like this before; but you have most likely experienced a situation where you 'just knew' what was going to happen, but you couldn't explain it to the people around you. Someone very wise once said, 'when we pray, we're talking to God. When we use our intuition, God is talking to us.' Our intuition is one of our higher faculties, but it's the one we tend to neglect the most because we are so used to living externally. We look to others for validation instead of utilizing that amazing power within ourselves to show us the way. Our thoughts work like radio frequencies; you tune into a station and you receive a signal back along with the message it carries. Your intuition works on a frequency, and it's usually on a higher frequency than your conscious thoughts.

Think back to a situation where someone told you to do something, and you knew it wasn't the right way to go. Something was tugging at you inside, telling you to go the other way, but you were afraid of being wrong so you took the other person's advice. When the results arrived, it turns out your gut feeling was right and you're now banging your head against the wall, wishing you had listened to yourself. Here's a little secret: these moments don't happen by chance. They don't occur at random, and your intuition isn't out of your control. Just like your imagination, you can develop it.

When you set a goal that is so big and so exhilarating, you're going to need your intuition to guide you because chances are the people around you have never been to where you want to go. Those conversations you have with yourself, that feeling in the pit of your stomach, listen to them! Your spiritual self knows exactly what you should do and it's giving you a signal by tapping into your subconscious mind and expressing itself in your body as a vibration. You know, we mentioned Kyle Cease earlier. Kyle has built his intuition to such a level, that he is confident enough to use it in making his business decisions. If he doesn't 'feel right' about a deal, he will walk away. If he does, he'll say yes and won't think twice. This process has worked out for the better every single time. The majority of this chapter is about a personal experience, and the reason for this is because no one can truly explain what your intuitive factor is all about. The next time your gut feeling kicks in, you'll know exactly what it's trying to tell you.

# How to Join Those Inside Conversations

Intuition is your ability to get in touch with the energy that surrounds you. You can literally read off the vibrations or frequencies of a person like a book when you develop this intelligence. This higher part of you also speaks to you in a non-verbal language, but you have to practice getting in tune with this factor. When we are talking to an audience, we can literally feel their energy; what they are feeling and thinking. If we catch on that they seem to be slipping away, we automatically do something to bring their focus back to what we're talking about. It's an absolutely amazing faculty! In order to use this to the best of your ability, you have to learn to trust it first. The next time you're about to make a decision, sit back and get in tune with what you feel like you should do, and then go out there and do it. When the results come back, figure out whether you went with your gut feeling or if you took action based on something else. Ask yourself for guidance every morning, relax your mind and body before any big event, and bring more of yourself to the surface.

PART III:

# Now Go Light Up
# The City

CHAPTER 10

# Eleven Million
# Kilowatt Hours

N aveed: *"The idea of surviving five days in military boot camp was sending chills down my spine. It seemed like an absolutely impossible job and I had no idea how I was going get through nearly a week of rigorous training. Two months prior to my departure for the camp, I faced a terrible accident where I tripped and skid across the pavement, an accident that damaged my knee for two months. On the day I left for camp, I was still limping and I couldn't help but think and worry about how I was going to participate in any of the activities: crawling on the ground, climbing up the ropes, etc. At that point I had nothing else to hold onto but my faith in knowing I was going to pull through. I kept imagining the last day and how I had successfully accomplished all my tasks before heading back home. There were two terrifying challenges I had yet to face, the thought of which I was dreading.*

*The first challenge consisted of walking up and down the steep slope of a giant hill, which was a two-mile journey. Still not being able to walk properly, I was thinking of ways to get out of it because I knew my right leg would break down half way up the hill. I went to one of the instructors in the military camp, and asked him if I could sit out this specific task and I explained my knee incident. He asked for proof in the form of a doctor's note, which I had not brought with me. The next day, the time had come for the terrifying challenge. I closed my eyes and imagined myself on top of the hill, piercing my flag into the ground, and heading back down. I whispered to myself, 'You can do this, you either do it or you don't.' I felt a strange, powerful energy around both my legs, arms and chest. My focus shifted to the top of the hill, and I was so completely determined that I wasn't thinking about anything else. It was silent even though I had close to eight hundred people talking around me and my eyes were still fixed on my destination. We were all placed in groups before the instructor blew the whistle as a starting signal, and my group was placed last to begin our way up. As I took the first few steps, I could feel my right knee shaking, as the muscles were still weak. I kept walking up, singing all kinds of songs to myself, and at one point I thought about how difficult it used to be for me to run in the park and how far I had come since then. My body was surging with more energy and I noticed that people who were fitter and much more muscular were sitting down for water breaks and resting their legs. I did not want to stop even for a second; I kept walking up like I was strolling around in a park. Before I knew it, I had reached my destination. The reality was just like what I had pictured in my mind; it was like Deja vu. I placed my colored flag in the ground and made my way back down. I was in shock and awe of how I accomplished something which seemed nowhere near possible just a few minutes ago.*

*Even though I was victorious on that first day, nothing could prepare me for our next challenge: the parachute training. When they took us onto the training sight, I saw a long tower-like structure made of wooden planks with built-in stairs for people to walk all the way up. To be fair, the officers announced to everyone that those who are afraid of heights and those who have heart problems can raise their hands and they will be taken to the side at the waiting area - no proof required. I probably went back and forth on it a hundred times, debating whether I should sit back on this one or go for it. Bear in mind, those who decided to go with the training did not have the option to back out; they were forced to jump off the top even if they didn't want to. I thought about that walk up the hill, where something impossible had become possible - and I decided to participate in the training. They suited us up with all the gear, gave us our helmets, and told us to form a line to head up the tower (which was exactly 34 meters high). My heart began pounding faster with excitement, and I kept telling myself, 'this isn't so bad and it's going to be an amazing experience.' As I kept going up, the people watching from the bottom looked smaller, and I was on the same level as the trees around me. I was still thinking it was not going to be as bad as I feared. That is, until I reached the top and everything and everyone on the ground looked tiny. My legs began to shake and I went into fight or flight mode. I saw several of my team mates being kicked and pushed off because they were refusing to jump, and seeing that was beginning to terrify me even more. I shut my eyes instantly, and saw myself enjoying a ride on a rollercoaster, and how it was okay to yell and scream the first time while enjoying the drop. As my turn arrived, I ran and jumped off like there was no tomorrow. Time suddenly froze as I was in midair; I felt butterflies in my stomach, yet the thought that I could possibly fall and die kept entering my mind. My heart was beating faster and faster, I yelled at the top of my lungs and decided to allow myself to just enjoy the fall. After what seemed like ages, I finally touched solid ground, once again feeling rewarded for my decision. If I could do it again, I would do it a hundred times over. Nothing can ever stop us, except our thinking and our perception about things.*

Would you let your circumstances and conditions stop you from doing what you have to do? What if you found out that you possessed the power to create anything you wanted, as long as you could visualize it in your mind? We are inclined to believe that you would use it to the best of your abilities. We have been conditioned since birth to live our life based on our sensory factors - we can see, hear, smell, taste, and touch. As long as we are corresponding with our material world, we definitely need our sensory factors. However, if we want to acquire something greater in life, we cannot rely on these sensory factors because whatever is going on outside of ourselves is all a manifestation or expression of someone else's creation. We look at what is going on outside, we listen to what other people tell us, and we formulate ideas of what can or can't be done based on that information. That literally is like a lid on the thoughts we are capable of originating within our mind. In order to achieve what we want, or create the results we desire, we must activate our creative faculties - our higher intellectual faculties: Memory, Intuition, Reason, Will, Perception, and Imagination. Think of them as a group of muscles in our body; as you keep working on them, they get stronger and stronger.

First, let's talk about memory. How many times have you heard people say, 'I have a bad memory?' The truth is that you do not have a bad memory - you simply have a weak memory. There are books that can literally teach you how to memorize an entire book as well as remember names and numbers. We have a strange way of remembering things, and there are tricks and techniques that you can use to develop this powerful faculty.

Next we have our intuitive faculty. Have you ever been in a situation where you listened to your 'gut feeling,' and things turned out all right? Or when things didn't turn out all right, you thought to yourself, 'I should've gone with my gut feeling?' We have an ingenious faculty within us that allows us to pick up vibrations and frequencies in the universe. We can literally force our mind to tap into the universal intelligence to figure out what we need to do in order to achieve what we desire. There is a non-verbal voice that will be speaking to you, and that is when you 'know' what resonates with you and what doesn't.

Then we have our reasoning factor, which is one of the most powerful faculties we possess, and one we use almost every second. It is through this faculty that we tap into the infinite. There is a power that flows into our consciousness and through our bodies. When this power flows into our consciousness, it has no form or shape; we have the ability to originate thoughts by creating pictures and putting them together in order to create an idea. We can accept or reject thoughts by putting this faculty to work. This faculty is one of the first ones that we develop as toddlers; it's the one we use to ask questions like 'why?' and 'how?'

Now let's talk about will. When you actively use your will, you have a tremendous power of concentration. Our sensory factors bring a massive amount of information into our conscious mind. With the use of our will, we can concentrate to the level where we clear our mind of all outside information, and focus on what's really important. The will to the mind is like a magnifying glass to the sun. With this faculty you can accelerate the power of thoughts and ideas to accomplish so much more in a shorter period of time. The French Emperor Napoleon Bonaparte had an incredible will, which was demonstrated by his ability to concentrate - in fact one of his famous lines was, 'I see only the objective. The obstacles must give way.'

Next, we have perception. When people look at a situation, they usually only look at one side of it - that's where arguments and disagreements usually originate. Think back to a time when you had an argument with someone, and you could not come to a conclusion. However, after thinking about it, you realized they were right from their point of view, as were you. There are always several points of view, and if we take them into consideration and try to understand them, we can start thinking about how we can accomplish something, rather than why we can't.

The last faculty that we possess is our imagination, which we discussed in chapter two. The imagination is more evident in children, simply because when we are in school we are conditioned to think that fantasizing is wrong and unproductive. However, if we begin to implement this faculty in our careers and personal life, we will have the ability to create a picture of what we want in our minds, and then proceed to manifest it in our physical world.

Understanding our higher faculties is pretty amazing, but applying them produces a result that is ten times more magical. People don't understand where miracles come from simply because they don't understand the laws of the universe. There is an invisible power which we all operate with, and the more you understand it, the more you will be able to create the miraculous results you have always wanted.

Understand this: not even the erudite scientist will be able to tell you what you are capable of doing. You have deep reservoirs of talent and ability within you. Did you know that your body is a mass of energy? The molecules in your body produce eleven million kilowatt hours per pound worth of energy, enough to light up a small town for nearly a week! Did you know your central nervous system is one of the most complex electrical systems in the entire universe, one that would make a super computer look like a toy? Your blood travels for hundreds of miles in passageways, and it gets rid of the old stuff in one sweeping change - and yet we hear people walking around, claiming they don't have enough energy. You don't get energy, you create energy; it comes from within. If you live your life going after your burning desire, you will produce an immense amount of energy from within - that's called living.

Earl Nightingale once said that, 'people tip toe through life, hoping to make it safely to death.' If you really think about that for a while, you will begin to understand exactly what he meant. Most people let outside circumstances dictate how they live their lives because they base their entire worldviews on what they see, hear, smell, taste, and touch. Begin using your higher faculties and live from the inside out. We are God's highest form of creation - and we have been given the creative faculties which allow us to create whatever it is we desire. We teach our clients to develop these mental faculties, and it literally closes the gap between what they want in life and how to go about manifesting it.

## How To Develop The 'Eleven Million Kilowatt Hours'

Your higher faculties allow your thoughts to embark on a journey from the conscious mind into the physical world through action. If you do not work on developing these higher faculties, you will never be able to provide yourself with results that you truly want.

## Memory

Let's dive into your memory. There are very few that have been gifted with 'photographic memory.' Many would disagree if you tell them they have the potential to develop such a skill. Those with a strong memory have actively been using that part of their mind so that part of the 'muscle' is strong. We all have different passions and are unique in our own ways; but ultimately we have been given the same intellect and we operate within the same laws. If you wish to develop your memory, start using tools, games and books to improve this faculty. *"The Memory Book"* by Jerry Lucas and Harry Lorayne is a great tool and provides some excellent insight into developing our memory.

## Will

Our will allows us to focus on one thing at a time; it works like a laser beam, rather than a flashlight. Exercising one's will is very simple; however, it requires discipline and consistency. Light a candle and stare at it for a few seconds. The first few times you try this, your concentration will last only a few seconds before your mind begins to wander. As you continue to practice, your level of concentration will increase profoundly. When you can concentrate on one thing, you can concentrate on anything.

## Imagination

The imagination is an extremely powerful force when used properly. You have the ability to travel through time and space, penetrate cosmic waves, bring back a thought from the future, and then manifest it into physical form. We have had this ability since childhood; but when we went to school our teachers told us to stop day dreaming, and we stopped using this faculty. When we were day dreaming and building beautiful pictures in our mind, we were letting our creativity flow. All you have to do is sit down in a quiet and comfortable place and begin getting in touch with what makes you feel absolutely amazing. Close your eyes and think about the life you desire; what kind of house do you see yourself living in? What type of friends do you want to have? Get in touch with what you really want and be true to yourself in the process.

## Perception

There is a law of polarity, which is also known as the law of opposites. If there is cold, there is hot, if there's an inside, there is an outside. When we take a look at a situation, we will usually think about it from one point of view, and we never really think about shifting our perspective. Here is an exercise you should do as often as possible: whenever you have a problem with something, write it down on a piece of paper and then put it down on a table somewhere near you. Then ask yourself, 'is the problem on the table or is it in me?' If you still feel there is a problem, write it down on a piece of paper again and repeat the process. Walk around and look at the paper from different angles until you start to realize that the problem is not in you, it's on the table. That gives you the liberty to go out and find solutions. Stop thinking about why things can't be done and think about how they can. You will always be looking at two sides of the same situation, and you now have the power to choose which side is more empowering for you.

## Reason

Our reasoning faculty allows us to choose the thoughts we wish to entertain; it allows us to create whatever we want. Here's the problem that most people face: they look at their results, such as their bank statements, and then they think about how much money they are free to spend based on that piece of paper. They begin to get emotionally involved with the idea and then they act based on that emotion. The universe reacts to your action, and your results manifest. A child looks at his or her grades and believes that that is who he/she is. They become emotionally involved with the negative image they have of themselves, and they continue to produce similar results. Now when using our reasoning mind, we can literally alter the course of our entire life by looking at our current results to simply know where we are, and then think about where we want to be instead. Our reasoning factor allows us to choose our thoughts, so we can begin to create, instead of fighting existing reality.

## Intuition

Our intuition is our ability to get in touch with the energy that surrounds us. As we discussed in the previous chapter, you can literally read the vibrations of a person like a book when you develop this type of intelligence. The more in tune you get with the other faculties, the more you will develop your intuitive factor.

This is truly the power we possess; no other species in the universe

NAVEED ASIF & SONIKA MADARASMI ASIF

has the power to tap into the infinite and create the life of their dreams. Make certain that you develop your higher self, and you will be able to produce anything you desire as long as you work in harmony with the laws of the universe.

CHAPTER 11

# Speak To The Light

*S*onika: *"In October 2014, I had one of the worst experiences of my life. I had just restarted my workout routine, and I chose to begin with an intense cardio workout. Fifteen minutes into the workout, I missed a step and slipped, and ended up with an ankle fracture in two places. The whole incident was such a blur that I was completely oblivious to the pain until I got to the hospital. I was told I needed surgery, and after a long, sleepless night, I was taken to the surgery ward where they placed a strip of metal and screws into my bone. The days that followed were excruciating, both mentally and physically. I was fighting the pain from the surgery every night, as well as trying to push away depressing and negative thoughts that left me thoroughly exhausted. As time went by, I began to realize that these moments would soon be over, and I will never get these 6 months back. So I began to work on my perception, and I began to constantly look for the good in every situation. Four months later, Naveed and I had an idea to start an online business, and because I had no choice but to sit in bed, I worked on our business day and night. Before I knew it, I had made more money online in one month than I had ever made in a year. It was astounding to see the results that manifested from the act of shifting and changing my perception. That experience left me with complete faith in the idea that everything depends on our thoughts and the way we look at things. If I hadn't allowed myself to make something good out of my otherwise horrible situation, I probably wouldn't have earned a single penny.*

We discussed the power of our higher faculties earlier in this book and how to develop them for our benefit. Perception is a key element involved in spiritual growth because whatever we focus on grows, while the other part falls away. The other part exists but it will not be visible to us. Bob Proctor once told us a story about how he was on stage giving a seminar, and he noticed a really negative vibration coming from a few people in the audience. He asked for advice, and realized that he simply had to 'speak to the light.' Positive and negative vibrations may be equally present in any given situation, but we have the ability to reason and choose what we want to give our focus to.

According to T. Harv Eker's article called 'Why We're Too Smart And Should Pretend We're Dogs,' there are three ways that we handle situations that aren't going our way: resistance, acceptance and utilization. Take a look at your pets at home, especially if you have a dog. No matter how hard you yell at your pet, it will always come back in the same manner, as if nothing happened. The dog won't lose its mind if it gets wet in the rain or hasn't been taken outside in time for its morning walk. The majority of us resist the situation that is occurring, setting ourselves up in a negative vibration, and ultimately messing up our entire day. You've probably heard the saying, 'what you resist, persists.' You're letting the universe know that you want more of this because you're reacting to it. After going through this rough patch, we finally learn to accept the situation the way it is. At this point you are starting to use your reasoning ability, and you're starting to really think about the situation for the first time. You are accepting it for what it is, and moving on. However, this doesn't make the situation any better or worse. Finally, a tiny 1% of the population will attempt to utilize the situation. Every time something occurs that is outside of their plan, they take it as a sign and figure out how to turn that incident to their benefit. They've successfully changed their paradigm and have learned to automatically search for the good in every single situation.

So why isn't everybody able to utilize negative situations? It's because we are used to receiving instant gratification. When we pay for something, or we take a certain action, we are in the habit of expecting to be rewarded right off the bat. Therefore, when a negative situation occurs, we aren't able to handle that situation effectively, and we engage in a series of negative reactions. According to the Law of Receiving, we must give good before we can receive it. As we mentioned earlier, there is a power that is flowing to and through us. Now as this power enters our consciousness, we build thoughts, but it's the kind of thoughts we build in that moment that will determine what thoughts we will receive in the future. Visualize a beautiful, lavender energy flowing in through the crown of your head. You take that energy and build a positive thought, and you send that thought out. As that energy leaves your conscious mind, there is an empty space; and because we attract like energy to us, that space in your consciousness fills up with the exact same type of energy that you sent out.

Our thoughts move at warp speed, so they circulate faster than material things. If we give some money to charity, it may take some time, but that money is eventually returned to us through a different channel. Riches are simply in the air, they are always circulating, and it works the same way with anything else you desire. This is the true reason that you reap what you sow, because you're attracting exactly what you send out. Start giving just to give; if your conscious mind is filled with 'getting,' what you want will never be attracted, simply because you haven't made space for it! It's an interesting concept to think about, as we end up sabotaging our own results.

## How to Speak to the Light

In order to truly be able to appreciate the good in every situation, there is one concept we must master; and that concept is called Gratitude. We've heard a lot about how we should be grateful for everything we have, but not many people truly utilize this amazing idea for their benefit. A lot of us try to be grateful by comparing ourselves to those who are less fortunate; if this is what you've been doing, then it's time to make a change. It's important to understand that everyone in this entire world has limitless potential to accomplish absolutely anything they put their mind to. The true power of gratitude lies in the vibration it sets up in your body. Take some time to think of a few things that you are truly grateful for, and impress them upon your subconscious mind. Really build the image of what you're grateful for in your mind and allow the feeling to spread throughout your body. You may find that this exercise sends chills and shivers down your spine. Wallace D. Wattles in his book 'The Science of Getting Rich', wrote, 'the whole process of mental adjustment and attunement can be summed up in one word, and that word is Gratitude.'

Make it a point to wake up every morning and make a list of ten things you are grateful for. As you write it down, allow yourself to get lost in the feeling that this exercise brings about. Try to make this list every day and you will find that this exercise gets harder and harder as you go along, simply because we are not in a habit of being grateful for the smallest things in life. When you're done, close your eyes and send love to three people that bother you. You will set up a reaction that will prove beneficial for you and for them. Lastly, ask your higher self for guidance for the day. When you turn these exercises into a habit, you will find that you have completely shifted your vibration, and you will have turned your external world into something absolutely beautiful and magnificent.

CHAPTER 12

# Opposites Don't
# Really Attract

**N**aveed: *"Around mid-January 2013, I went out with my friends to a
Hookah Bar. I was definitely in no mood to party that night, but my friends
insisted so I decided to go along. When I found a place to sit down after reaching the
venue, I recognized one or two familiar faces that were outside of my regular crowd.
However, there was a girl there who was having the time of her life. After ten years of
meeting up with the same group of friends, I had never seen her around. I nudged one
of my friends to ask who that girl was and if she was from abroad. They got us both
introduced and we shook hands with a simple 'Hi'. We didn't really speak the rest
of the night.*

*Two weeks later my friends and I made plans to go out partying, and the same
girl showed up. After chatting with one another, we could gather that we both enjoyed
each other's company. After getting home, I wanted to keep talking to her, so I added
her on Facebook. The first time we began chatting online we couldn't stop talking to
one another and it just felt right. We knew shortly after that we wanted to spend
more time together, and we spoke to one another every chance we got. A few months
later, we began dating and we discovered something absolutely mind-boggling as we
shared our past experiences. We discovered that we not only shared mutual friends for
years, but we'd also been attending the same concerts, festivals, and wedding parties -
yet we never ran into one another. Turns out she had met my friends at every event,
but she never ran into me. We came to the conclusion that we only crossed paths
because we were in the right place at the right time. Though we were both only in our
early 20s, we knew this was it for us. Our parents saw how happy we were and they*

*suggested we get married. Prior to meeting her I would've definitely had an objection, simply because I always wanted to be 'well off and settled financially' before taking on the responsibility of marriage. My love for her was much greater than that old idea I had, which is why I decided to listen to myself and go for it. I knew right away that my decision was the right one. I wasn't panicked either, in fact I had never felt more relaxed about the idea of getting married.*

*As soon as we agreed to get married, we began talking about the wedding: the hall we would love to get married in, the outfits, the dates - every possible detail. Furthermore, we began living like it had already happened; we spoke about how awesome it would be and how much fun everyone would have. We fell in love with the idea so much that we knew deep down that everything would go smoothly. Now bear in mind, I have a Muslim background while my wife, Sonika, has a Hindu background. The opposition began in our communities shortly after they heard the 'announcement' that we were getting married. We heard several stories about people being afraid that the marriage wouldn't last because apparently people from two different religious backgrounds can never stay together in harmony. People had issues with our age, and the difference in our financial statuses. In an Indian society, traditional culture is usually everything and people either follow the rules or they get ridiculed. Sonika and I, however, kept looking at our dream wedding and focused on those who supported us. We shut out all opposition and didn't let it have any effect on our decision.*

*We had two months to prepare our outfits, venues, DJs, wedding planners, etc. Usually, for Indian weddings, people prepare one year ahead of time, simply because there's so much that goes into it. We truly believed that everything would work out the way we imagined it would. We called all the hotels that we really wanted to book for the wedding but they were all full due to short notice; but that didn't stop us from dreaming about the ballroom we really wanted. We chose to ignore the fact that every hotel was booked and we kept the image of our favorite hotel in mind. We imagined them calling us to tell us that the January 10th would be available for us after all. In December, we got a call from the hotel and they told us that there was a last minute cancellation on that very date and the ballroom was available for us. We weren't even surprised because we were just focusing on the amazing opportunity that lay ahead.*

*After getting married, we wanted to improve our lives and take our financial life to a whole new level. I was working with my dad at the time in the textile business but I wasn't moving ahead because I wasn't passionate about it. Sitting around in our spare time, Sonika and I decided to watch the hit movie 'The Secret,' because we needed a boost of inspiration to start something big. After watching the movie, I was still not seeing any significant changes even though I knew that the concept of the law of attraction made sense. Days would pass by and our results wouldn't change and I* *was beginning to get quite frustrated. One evening Sonika and I came across Bob Proctor's seminar video on YouTube, and when we heard him speak, we knew right away the information in the video would change our lives. For several days we kept watching his videos over and over and suddenly something clicked; we realized that the reason we weren't able to attract big opportunities and big money was not because the law of attraction works selectively, but because our minds were not in tune with getting the results we wanted with respect to success and money. We began to work on our mindset right away, and we put up a huge vision board in our room, filling it with all our dreams and wants for the next 3 years. One of our main components consisted of a $1 bill, to which we added 6 zeroes with a magic marker. We had no idea how to create that amount, but it didn't matter - we knew we wanted it.*

*Now at this moment something extraordinary happened – but let's start off with a little context. A few years ago my family and I began working on a case to distribute several assets based on the will of my grandmother. The challenging aspect of it was that the three families that were involved, including mine, were not able to communicate with one another effectively. Interestingly enough, after we put up the 'million-dollar bill' on our vision board and believed we had already acquired it, situations and circumstances began to change. Out of nowhere, we were approached by a law firm that specialized in handling difficult cases like ours. Because of this new opportunity, everyone began agreeing and working in harmony with one another. I started seeing a dramatic shift in everyone's attitude; there was fairness and clear communication between the families and the law firm. In order to settle and finish the deal, my family and I agreed to give this firm the power of attorney to handle the case. As we were approached by the lawyer to sell the first property, we had brokers and buyers personally visiting us to find out if all the shareholders were interested in selling, since they had heard that the family dispute had been going on for few years. As we did our research and found the best buyers, we had pushed the price beyond the market bidding price. Every single professional broker and expert told us that the minimum price we had given was absurd, as no one had ever sold a similar piece of land at that price before in the entire country. We didn't care about what others believed; we knew this piece of land would sell for the minimum price we had put up. We kept living as though the land was already sold for the price we desired, and spoke to buyers and brokers that met us as though it had already happened. One day, our lawyer called to tell us that he had found a buyer who was willing to buy at the price we had put up and all the shareholders agreed to accept the deal that was on the table and walk away winners. Turns out that this property was sold at the highest price ever in the history of Thailand, and the details were published in the Bangkok Post. So there it was: Sonika and I had attracted two million dollars, double the amount of money we had put up on our vision board.*

Everything that is going on in our lives (the people we meet, the places we go, and the causes of our health) consist of people/things/events which we are attracting into it. The law of attraction is always working - whether you understand it or not. In '*The Secret*', it is explained very well that the law of attraction is always working based on what we want in life and whether our emotions are in line with what we desire. The one big thing missing from the movie is the fact that the law of attraction is a secondary law; the primary law is the law of vibration. It is the law that everything on the planet is operating within. The law of vibration decrees that everything moves, nothing rests, and that we live in an ocean of motion. If you look at your body under a microscope, you will see your cells moving at a high speed of vibration right before your eyes. The word emotion, as we know it, is a word used to describe the conscious awareness of the vibration our body is in. Our brain is an electronic switching station that has a positive charge and negative charge. When we have a positive idea, our brain fires a positive charge throughout our entire body, which puts the body in a positive vibration - the same goes with a negative idea. We attract literally anything that is in harmony with our vibration. We operate exactly the way radio does; we operate on frequencies. When we have a thought and we impress that thought onto our subconscious mind, we alter the amplitude of vibration in our brain, which puts the entire body in the same frequency. There is really a science to getting rich, to being abundant in all areas of life. As long as you understand how the laws of the universe operate, you will be able to be, do, and have anything you want. That is a guarantee for every single person, every single time.

## How To Correctly Use The Law Of Attraction

The law of attraction is such a simple law, yet so powerful and very much misunderstood. Most people create vision boards and think about what they want, hoping for the things they want to manifest. If you want to attract the good that you desire into your life, you are going to have to understand the law the way Ralph Waldo Emerson understood it: 'You do not attract what you want, you attract who you are.' So how do we attract what we want into our lives? What you want to do is to get totally relaxed and sit and think about what you want; visualize it, see yourself in possession of it until you can feel it, taste it, smell it, hear it. Then take out a piece of paper and write it down in the present tense,

'*I am so happy and grateful now that*_____. As you write it down and see yourself in possession of what you desire, be grateful, as though you already have it. Make sure to take the card with you everywhere you go and keep it lose in your pocket or purse, because every time you touch it you will see the flash of an image of what you want on the screen of your mind. When that happens, you become more and more emotionally involved with what you want, a process that will turn simple wishes into a burning desire. You will begin acting as if you already have what you want and that will cause you to be in the right frequency, where you will attract the thoughts, circumstances, or people into your life to help you turn your vision into a physical reality.

# CHAPTER 13

# It's Your Life

The majority of people waste their lives following the crowd, simply because they are afraid to pay the price for being different. The best way to begin this chapter is to look at a quote by Bob Proctor: 'For most people, when their hearts stop beating it is just a formality, because they never truly lived.' People are so focused on conforming to society and what others expect of them that they forget to focus on what they want. If you want to create something big in your life, it takes courage. According to Earl Nightingale, the opposite of courage isn't cowardice; it's conformity.

When you wake up in the morning, what's the first thing you think about? Do you think about your family? Do you think about your job? Are your thoughts empowering or disempowering? Our habits tell us a great deal about why our results are the way they are. You've got to find that burning desire, one that will keep you going no matter what obstacles come in your way. If you can see the image in your mind, you can hold it in your hand, because everything is created twice.

When we began our journey in the personal development industry, we had no idea what price we had to pay, or the actions we would need to take to succeed. All we cared about was following the best of the best, and doing exactly what they did. With every opportunity that arose, we found a way to jump up and grab it right away, a habit that tripled our results in an amazingly short period of time. Our desire to help people grow and manifest the life of their dreams is the one picture that replays in our minds over and over, day in and day out. If someone were to ask us today if we were willing to do whatever it took to reach our goals, our answer would be an unequivocal 'YES!' This is because we don't focus on what could go wrong on our journey; we focus on what is going right and we build upon that every single day.

Start asking yourself questions that you're too afraid to answer - these are the questions that will really help you figure out where you're going wrong. What do you really want to do? What makes you happy? Where do you want your life to be in the next 6 months? Explain and write out every single detail on a piece of paper, and make that image so crystal-clear that you can paint the same image in someone else's mind. Allow the feeling of already achieving this dream to fill your body and express itself in everything you say and do. You know, we make space for a lot of things in life, but we don't make space for the one or two big things that would truly make us happy. If you're looking for someone to come work for you, setup a desk with papers, a telephone and a cup of coffee; in due time, you'll have someone sitting behind that desk. If you're looking for the love of your life, start living like you're already with them. Write letters to them, imagine yourself spending time with them, and talk to them on a daily basis. Remember, it doesn't matter what anyone else thinks, this is about what *you* truly want!

You've got an immense amount of talent and potential lying dormant within you; and it's going to take some serious passion and desire to ignite that flame. Aim for something so big that you have no choice but to pull out something inside of you to make it happen. It's like going skydiving for the first time: you're aware of potential dangers, but you know the rewards are massive, and you have no choice but to trust yourself and in your ability to jump off that plane. When you're working towards a goal that you don't know how to reach you're *alive*. You've got direction, you've got persistence, you've got courage - but most of all, you have faith. Listen to your intuition and notice every little thing that comes into your life. The people, situations and opportunities that occur are telling you something about your state of mind - use this to your benefit.

## How To Attract The Person of Your Dreams

According to *The Secret*, you've got to fill yourself up before you can give to someone else. Those who look for a partner to make them feel better about themselves will never have a fulfilling relationship, because they aren't able to reciprocate and give back to their partner.

The law of attraction is actually a secondary law. The primary law is the law of vibration, which states that everything moves and nothing rests. We live in an ocean of motion. Our thoughts are at a certain frequency, and create a certain vibration in our body. Due to this vibration, we take certain actions. The universe *reacts* to our action, ultimately determining our results. The universe's reaction may consist of the opportunities that come to you, or the people you attract into your life. If your thoughts are positive and you are completely fulfilled with yourself, you will attract a person who is in the same thought frequency as you! Your spirits are truly expressing themselves, that's what we call 'a match made in heaven,' or more commonly referred to as 'soul mates.' You can only attract to yourself what vibrates in harmony with you!

There is a difference between being in a habit of having someone around as compared to loving them. With love there is only energy, and this energy ultimately manifests in our physical world as a loving relationship. If your relationship is not up to par, or you have been attracting the wrong people into your life, it is time to evaluate this loving energy.

To attract a loving relationship into your life, you have got to believe that this desire has already come true. Only when you believe in your mind that you are worthy of this relationship will it manifest in your physical world. Take a piece of paper and draw a circle. In the middle of the circle write the words 'my perfect man' or 'my perfect woman.' Draw lines coming out of the circle and write down the exact qualities that you want this person to possess. Read it every day, and live like you have already attracted this person! But remember, we cannot add the face of someone we know to this image, because we will then be playing with this person's mind. Let the universe worry about who is right for you, you just focus on what you WANT. Write down this affirmation: 'I love everything about myself, and therefore I attract to myself people who love everything about me, and whom I love in return.' You will begin to see that people will respond to you differently, it is absolutely amazing!

To rekindle an old relationship, it requires the energy of love and gratitude. Negative energy within a relationship only leads to more of the same. There is a law of polarity in the universe, in that everything has an opposite. If there are negative aspects of your loved one, the exact opposite exists as well. It's only a matter of whether or not they are expressing that side of themselves. In order to allow this expression, take a pen and paper, and write down ten things you love about your partner. Do this morning and night, every single day. The energy of gratitude that you give off will automatically come back to you, causing your loved one to express the side of him or herself that is in harmony with the energy that you give off!

The Bible's Book of Matthew offers us these words: 'Ask and it shall be given to you; seek, and ye shall find; knock and it shall be opened unto you. And all things, whatsoever ye shall ask in prayer, believing, ye shall receive.'

James Allen, in his book *As a Man Thinketh*, wrote: 'Mind is the master power that molds and makes.' You've got control of your life, including your relationship. Repeat this affirmation: 'I am in a loving relationship, filled with love, trust and respect.'

# How to Create & Attract Multiple Sources of Income

Multiple sources of income, also known as MSIs, are what separate the rich from the wealthy. A lot of people in the world today view MSIs as 'extra effort' or an increased investment of time and money, and that's why 96% of the population is constantly working to produce a substantial income. Go ahead and repeat this phrase 3 times: 'Money is easy to earn.'

Now that you've got your mind prepared for what's to come, it's important to understand what money really is. So let's think about what money actually is? Well in very basic terms, money is the reward you receive for rendering a service. In fact, broken down even further, money is simply just an idea. That piece of paper in your wallet holds no value unless you link a value to it, and this value is different depending on your relationship to money and wealth. The late Mike Todd said, 'Being broke is a temporary situation. Being poor is a mental state.' To increase your income, it is important to have a good relationship with money; if you are struggling it's because you are not successfully allowing money to flow into your life. Poverty is bold and ruthless. It will rear its ugly head at every point possible and come charging into your life. Riches are shy and timid; they have to be attracted. There exists a stream of power in life. One side of the stream carries you to wealth, while the other carries you to poverty. The side that carries you to wealth consists of positive thoughts: faith, belief, willingness and the like. The side that carries you to poverty consists of negative thoughts: fear, anger, impatience, and so on. It is possible to propel yourself from one side of the stream to the other, but you've got to change the root cause of your financial statement. That root cause lies in the depths of your consciousness. You need to begin by creating powerful, prosperity-conscious ideas in your mind, and you need to keep them alive by getting emotionally involved with them. You need to love money, and it will love you back.

## There are three categories of Money: we'll call them M1, M2 and M3.

M1 consists of those who are trading time for money, which is how the majority of people today are earning their living. You get up in the morning, you go to work, and you come home. You repeat this process for 30 days and then you get a cheque at the end of the month. Here's the problem with this category: you're going to eventually run out of time. It's inevitable; your income is capped because of the clock. Now you can be rich by being in this category, but only at the expense of other things in life that you love.

M2 consists of those who invest money for money. This is made up of approximately 3% of our population. You can make a large amount of money in this category, but not without investing a significant amount of time looking for an advisor, planning, investing, waiting and then receiving an income. Eventually you need to accumulate enough to invest in something else. Very few people are in this category simply because very few people have got money to invest.

M3 consists of that tiny 1% of the population that is earning millions and millions of dollars' worth of income from multiple sources. This category is made up of people who are multiplying their time for money. You simply set up a product or service that you can offer in an automated version without you having to be around, or duplicate yourself and delegate jobs, and you've set up a source of income that doesn't require any more effort. And then you go on to create some more. This is what separates the wealthy from the rich.

Now here's something that not many people will tell you. The best way to earn an income is to help others. That has been taught and proven over and over again. The more services you provide, the bigger the reward. Marketing tactics are applying this very technique by becoming solutions to problems that a lot of people face. But when you provide true, heart to heart service, your rewards and compensation are going to skyrocket.

The key ingredient to increasing your income to the level of those you admire is growth. But not just growth on a conscious level, as you can get that from picking up any book. You need growth on a spiritual level; you've got to pull on something inside of you that you didn't even know was there.

The first step requires us to increase our awareness about ourselves and the industry we want to master. As we do this, we begin to increase the flow of ideas that are coming in from the universe. You've tuned into a higher frequency and you're getting all the ideas you need. Next, you've got to make that decision. Choose an idea that you really love and break out of your comfort zone to work towards it. Stick with the idea regardless of fear, and eventually the fear disappears. As you go through trial and error, you learn to respond to your environment instead of just reacting to it, because you have faith in yourself and the service you are providing. Last but not least you need to learn to give it your all until you become an absolute Master, and you are compensated for your knowledge and efforts along with your service. As you look at the service you are providing, ask yourself, 'what can I do differently? 'How do I make this better?' What else can I create as another way to render service and increase my income?' That flow of ideas will enter your consciousness, and you've got to start the whole process all over again, but this time, you're going in with experience, which is the 6$^{th}$ level of awareness. Imagine the time you save after becoming a Master! With every new idea you're growing, you're doing something new, you're getting inspired and you never stop.

Now here's something not many people will tell you about building your income. Before you can start getting creative and investing major time and money into your passion, you've got to have your needs covered. This is extremely important! You have got to have your basic needs covered. If you are struggling to cover your basic needs, you first need to figure out a way to create something that you can eventually automate into a monthly source of income, so you can focus on creation and mastery in areas that you love. We encourage you to read the first chapter of Bob Proctor's *You Were Born Rich* called 'Me and Money.' Bob provides an absolutely brilliant solution to those who are struggling to pay off their debts.

There is no limit to the number of MSIs you create. The more the better! Start becoming prosperity conscious and get going! Here's an affirmation to repeat everyday: 'I am so happy and grateful now that money flows to me in increasing quantities through multiple sources on a continuous basis.'

## How to Achieve Your Perfect Health And Weight

We discussed earlier about how we self-sabotage our results without realizing it. This leads to the vicious cycle of seeing that number on the scale rise and fall without any understanding as to why it is happening. The real reason behind this up and down wave of motion lies in the treasury of our subconscious mind. Our body is programmed and we operate based on a paradigm. Now one part of our paradigm is our self-image, and this is the part that controls the thoughts and beliefs we have about ourselves.

Our perfect weight can only manifest if we make our desired result our comfort zone! In other words, make yourself feel uncomfortable until you get there. You've got to change your approach towards achieving that goal; and to change that you've got to change our self-image.

If we picture ourselves as a fat person, we will diet for a while, get comfortable, and without realizing it, our cybernetic mechanism will bring us right back to where we were. We cry, we get angry and eventually we give up! We need to treat the source. If our self-image doesn't change, we will never find the confidence, desire and persistence to succeed and manifest those results. Start writing that script of yourself being at your perfect weight. Use words like 'healthy,' 'fit,' and 'releasing weight.' Be careful not to self-sabotage by using phrases like 'losing weight' and 'dieting.' Surround yourself with a positive and live like you are already the size you want to be. Fill your closet with clothes that you want and picture that number on the scale; you no longer need to force yourself to do things you don't want to do!

Now let's get into physical health. There are a lot of people today involved in holistic healing, which involves treating the person as a whole: mind, body and spirit. Now there is a basic law of the universe that says, 'create or disintegrate' If you are not allowing your spirit to express and grow outside of your comfort zone, you're going to move backwards both mentally and, eventually, physically. If you are experiencing physical discomfort, or you simply wish to live a healthy and prosperous life, think deeply about how you approach your outside world. Do you look more to others for advice? Do you believe in your own abilities? If not, here is an affirmation for you to read every day, until this belief turns into a habit: 'I am the creator of my world. I have infinite potential and power within me to attract to me the good that I desire.'

# This Is Just The Beginning

We do things based on what logic tells us, and we do a great job at it because everything we do over a period of time becomes part of our paradigm. You are reading this book because you want to create a quantum leap in your results, which comes through application of knowledge and understanding. Reading this book once or twice will raise your level of awareness, but it may not improve your results to a significant degree unless you take the ideas in this book - even if they only constitute a paragraph - and study them over and over again until you have internalized them and taken action. It's the same principle we've seen countless times in our lives. When someone you know was given a math equation to solve and they didn't understand it, they had to maybe get a tutor to explain the question two or three times until something finally clicked. 'Oh now I get it!' Reading this book several times doesn't mean the content will change before your eyes, but you will continue to discover new things about yourself. Repetition truly increases our level of conscious awareness.

We encourage you to put the principles given to you in this book to the test by doing exactly what we have told you, without fail, for thirty or maybe even sixty days. When your paradigm changes, so will your logic, perception, level of creativity, and even how effective you are as a person. Most people are reluctant to really make a significant change in their lives, even after receiving certain principles such as the ones presented in this book; they go back to living the way they've always lived. People aren't really living their lives the way they truly want to. Use that marvelous tool in your mind, your imagination, and build beautiful pictures in your mind of how you really want to live, of who you want to become, and then use the ideas given to you in this book to help you create the life of your dreams. If you are going after what you really want, it must be something that scares you and excites you at the same time. You are God's highest form of creation and there is no limit to what you can do. We used the exact principles to create a major shift in our own lives and now we have shared this gift with you. It's YOUR life – and it's YOUR responsibility to make the necessary changes to achieve the results you desire.

# Acknowledgements

Writing a book to spread transformative information out into the world is one of the most enlightening experiences we've ever had. But completing this book would not have been possible without a team. By team, we mean all the minds and souls that have been connected with us in creating this powerful masterpiece that holds jewels of wisdom. Before making our acknowledgments, we had several ideas running through our minds of what to say, but as we began writing, we couldn't find the words to express our gratitude towards everyone who has been a part of our life and success.

We would like to acknowledge our parents, family, and relatives who have always shown so much love, and given all the warm support that anyone could ever hope for. Thank you for providing us with the space, encouragement, and giving us the wings to sore as high as we can today. We would like to acknowledge our mentor, Mr. Bob Proctor, who has given us an abundance of information that will live with us and now the thousands or hopefully millions of people that will be reading this book; and thank you for always pushing and always getting the best out of us every single day. We would like to thank Sandy Gallagher, who has worked side by side with Bob Proctor for several years now and has inspired us to grow as people as much as she has. We would like to thank the Proctor Gallagher Institute team and staff, Tracy, Chris, Gina, Becca, and Doug, who together always provided great service and support whenever we had questions or needed help.

We would like to acknowledge our teacher, without whom we would've never thought to write our book this way or even have had the courage to write any book at all, Peggy McColl.

Thank you Rob Riopel for always encouraging and extending your help whenever we had questions about creating business plans and structure, and referring us to Jason Chechik. Thank you Jason for being an incredible friend and a great marketing consultant for our website, business, and giving us so many amazing ideas.

We have to thank Success Resources and T. Harv Eker for providing great seminars - such as the Guerrilla Business Intensive and Millionaire Mind Intensive – which have given us multiple ideas in expanding our awareness in business, which played a great part in helping us to create this book.

Lastly, we would like to thank our friends, who have always added many colors to our lives and have always been with us during our worst and greatest times.

# Resources

Naveed & Sonika's Collection of Motivation and Programs to
Help You Live Your Life The Way It's Meant to Be Lived

"It's up to you to make your life what you want it to be.
Remember... It's Your Life!"
- Naveed & Sonika

Thinking Into Results is designed in such a unique way, that it provides an amazing experience for:

- An Individual: Your individual, personal goals and desires.
- A corporation: A complete corporate experience that leaves everyone with the impression of increase and motivation.
- A family: An experience that takes your family and personal relationships to a new level.

About The Program

Bob Proctor

Sandy Gallagher

Transforming the lives of millions around the world.

*Thinking into Results* is one-of-a-kind system based on 50 years of intensive research into the science and mechanics of personal achievements: what really makes successful people successful. Developed by world-renowned success expert Bob Proctor and legendary corporate attorney Sandy Gallagher, **it is the most powerful process EVER created for quickly and permanently transforming ANY goal, dream, or desire into reality.**

What You'll Get In This Phenomenal Program

- In-depth individual lessons focus intensively on a single essential element of the achievement process, with each lesson building upon the insights of the last.

- Your very own participant's workbook to challenge you to immediately apply what you learn, so you see and feel yourself changing, progressing, and moving closer to your goal in real time.

- A goal card that fits in your wallet for you to carry around in your pocket at all times.

- 12 Dynamic DVDs viewed twice a day, morning and evening, motivate you and reinforce the lesson content at multiple levels of consciousness — a critical key to achieving change quickly and making it permanent.

- Live coaching/consulting webinar sessions, 60-90 minutes every week, giving you the support, encouragement, answers, and expert guidance you need to keep moving forward on your journey to achievement.

Visit www.naveedsonika.com/thinking-into-results-sign-up to be a part of this amazing program!

Naveed & Sonika
COACHING

# Personal Mentoring

## With Naveed & Sonika, Your Results Will Become Inevitable

Every successful person has had a mentor. You may have one, or have had one in the past; but there is a big difference between a good mentor, and a GREAT mentor. Great mentors are 100% invested in getting their mentees to succeed. Their life purpose is to pass along the information in order for the mentee to be responsible for his/her own success! A great mentor believes you are capable of things that you don't even believe in yourself. With Naveed & Sonika, you won't just find a set of great mentors. You will find a legacy of information, passed down from 4 great mentors!

Andrew Carnegie, still known as one of the richest men who ever lived, passed on his wisdom to Napolean Hill. Napolean Hill created millions of millionaires through his book, "Think and Grow Rich", and in turn mentored Earl Nightingale who was the best recording artist of his time. Earl Nightingale eventually paired with Lloyd Conant to propel the personal development industry into existence in the 1960's. Bob Proctor spent 5 amazing years working with these individuals. After being trained and mentored by Bob, who is known today as a master in human potential and growth, Naveed & Sonika have the privilege and absolute pleasure, of passing this information into your hands. Naveed & Sonika have had the pleasure of seeing their clients flourish and transform before their very eyes; and nothing makes them happier than to be able to do the same for many others around the world.

**This program includes:**

- Personal one-on-one coaching
- Can be done in person, over the phone or online
- 60-90 minute sessions
- FREE access to our best-selling Thinking Into Results program
- Direct access and freedom to call us whenever you need it
- The most powerful information you've ever heard
- Permanent change in every area of your life
- A new-found desire and understanding of goal-achieving
- Complete clarity on how the mind works
- A never-seen-before image of the mind

Visit www.naveedsonika.com/free-consultation for a free session and see how you can get personally mentored by Naveed & Sonika!

## Connect With Us!

naveedsonikacoaching      naveed.sonika

naveedsonika      Naveed and Sonika Coaching

To contact us:

**Visit us:** www.naveedsonika.com
**Call Us:** +66(89)5067076, +66(86)1074578
**Skype Us:** naveedsonikacoaching
**Email Us:** support@naveedsonika.com

**Mail Us:**
Naveed & Sonika Coaching Co., Ltd
54/7 Mooban Aree
Sukhumvit soi 26, Klong Toey
Bangkok, Thailand 10110

Naveed & Sonika Coaching Co., Ltd

**PGI** CERTIFIED CONSULTANT
*Turn Thinking Into Results*

www.ingramcontent.com/pod-product-compliance
Lightning Source LLC
Chambersburg PA
CBHW060644150426
42811CB00079B/2335/J